Z 00

THE TRAVELLERS' LIBRARY

★

DOG AND DUCK

THE TRAVELLERS' LIBRARY

Uniform with this volume

DOG AND DUCK
A LONDON CALENDAR
ET CÆTERA

by

ARTHUR MACHEN

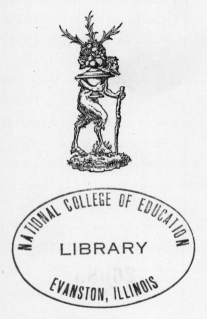

LONDON
JONATHAN CAPE 30 BEDFORD SQUARE

FIRST PUBLISHED 1924
FIRST ISSUED IN THE TRAVELLERS' LIBRARY 1926

PRINTED IN GREAT BRITAIN

CONTENTS

DOG AND DUCK

NOT long ago, I remember reading that a Stool Ball match had been played at Lord's Cricket Ground. I said to a man I know, a person learned in games:

'What is Stool Ball? Is it the same thing as Knurr and Spell?'

He rebuked my ignorance. He explained the two games. He explained further that even to hit the ball at Knurr and Spell a man must be northern born. He said it was one of the most difficult games that had ever been invented.

But this is merely by the way; it is an illustration of the fact that many of the old English games linger on, half-forgotten, played vehemently perhaps; but only by a few initiates.

So I dare say that many of my readers will not even have heard of the game of Dog and Duck. Yet, within ten minutes' walk of Lord's, the faithful few know where to find the headquarters of the M.D.D.C. — the historic Alley of the Marylebone Dog and Duck Club.

At first sight, entering the alley, one would say that here was a quiet London garden, of the

7

BOCARDO

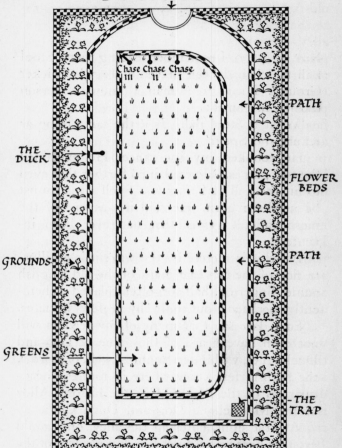

PATH

THE DUCK

FLOWER BEDS

PATH

GROUNDS

GREENS

THE TRAP

Chase III Chase II Chase I

old-fashioned kind, with an old-fashioned house at the back of it. Roughly, the extent of the alley – which includes, as I shall presently explain, the 'Grounds' and the 'Greens' – is twenty yards by ten. It is overhung by old trees and ivy-covered walls, and seems the very place for an old-world game. Bowls, once the favourite game of the clergy and of dignified and elderly persons generally, used to be played in just such surroundings. And Dog and Duck, like Bowls, is a game for the leisurely, a game of amenities.

I said the alley was like a garden. Well, imagine a lawn, shaped somewhat like a capital D. About it goes what we may call the garden path, this is the actual alley. On the right hand are flower beds – the 'grounds' – and to right and left the path is separated from grounds and greens by tiles: these are the 'walls.'

Note one point. You entered by a door, which may be imagined to be in the middle of the top of the D. Here the alley widens to right and left, making a sort of bay in front of the door. This space, marked off by a white line, is called 'Bocardo,' in humorous allusion to a mode of the Fourth Figure in Scholastic Logic. If you got into this figure, you had considerable difficulty in getting out again, in getting back into the more natural first figure. There used to be a prison at Oxford called Bocardo. Facing Bocardo, the lawn, or greens, is marked off by three posts. These are the three 'chaces,' or scoring marks.

Now, suppose you are standing in the middle of the green, watching a match at Dog and Duck. The first man to play — 'first troller' as he is called — stands in the alley on a slightly raised platform, two feet square, at the right-hand bottom corner of the D. The right foot must be on the platform — 'the trap'; the left foot on the alley behind. He takes the ball, which is a hollow india-rubber ball of two inches diameter, and begins the 'bump': a bump is the delivery of five balls in succession. His object is to bowl, or serve, the ball on the alley as far as possible round the top of the D. If the ball rests between chaces one and two, he scores five. If it rests between the second and third chace, he scores ten. If it turns the corner and rests in the return alley, the troller's score is twenty. If it passes the Duck which marks the fourth chace, the player scores forty.

But there are penalties and difficulties. The ball must not leave the alley. It may, indeed, skim on the edge of the tiles, or walls; but if it touches the earth on the right, or the lawn at the left, for a moment, the umpire, standing in the middle of the lawn, calls out 'grounds' or 'greens,' and the scorer deducts five from the player's total: 'lack five.'

Then, there is Bocardo. The ball that stays within the white line which marks Bocardo fails to score.

Here then, are the two great difficulties of the game. The tyro, a cricketer, possibly, possibly a distinguished amateur of bowls, smiles in a superior way as he takes his stand on the trap. He is to bowl a child's ball round a garden path. Very good! and then, to his astonishment, the ball has jumped 'walls,' and is revelling in 'grounds,' or more rarely is disporting itself on the lawn.

The fact is that a ball, with sufficient force behind it to round the left-hand corner of the D and score twenty, is apt, save in the hands of the most skilful players, to 'break alley,' to 'go to earth,' as that famous old professional, Harry Gunter, used to put it. It takes the best part of a lifetime to learn how to impart that peculiar swirling motion to the ball which will carry it down the alley, cause it to impinge on the right wall at exactly the right angle, and then 'bring it low,' make it come round the D close to the top wall, and at last swing it triumphantly round the corner, perhaps to Chace IV, the Duck, and a score of forty.

The supercilious beginner comes to grief over walls; Bocardo is the terror of the experienced player. Old James Henry Messiter, who invented the 'railway service,' used to groan and say that 'Bocardo beats all.' A ball may be well held, well placed, well played, well bungled, and yet some infinitesimal error at the last moment may spoil everything. It may be only the variation of a hundredth of an inch in the ball's position as it leaves the player's fingers. But look, it swings down the alley, a free, a gallant ball; it impinges on the wall low down at the exact spot which the player has marked for it; and then, instead of coming down low it rolls up and abides placidly in Bocardo, and, as Dickens says of another game, the player's score is as blank as his face.

Bocardo lies in wait for every good player, no matter what his service may be. I have seen it bring low the hopes of a distinguished Prebendary of the Church who had studied Dog and Duck under Messiter; and I have seen it foil a well-known actor, who fancied himself extremely, as the sole possessor of the secret of Jack Toplady's 'straight slows.'

Toplady, by the way, was the only player who was ever able to score consistently with the 'white ball.' This, it may be explained, is the ball which never touches 'walls' at all, to left or right, but wheels round the curve of the D in a perfect orbit. Old players who have seen Toplady at work, have assured me that these white balls of his looked as if they were running in tapes.

The game of Dog and Duck — sometimes, in earlier days, known as Chase Mallard — makes its rare appearances in our literature. So far as I know, there has been no scientific treatise on the sport; but there are some odd allusions to it scattered up and down in old half-forgotten books. Thus, in modernized English, the mediæval poet, traditionally known as Nicholas Scrope — his identity is uncertain — in his *House of Mirth*:

When men in their dalliance
Would have of mirth some pastance,
Then go they to a fair ground,
With the green tree well set around,

And green grass in abundance
To a place that is a gay pleasaunce.
And there is a pathway measured well,
This is their alley, as they tell.
And so with ball in place of bow,
They chase the mallard that may not go
One jot or whit from his station,
But abideth still in his fashion.
But though alway his stand be stable,
Yet is that ball most variable,
And departeth sudden from his right way
And all gates ever will stray;
Till men cry out, 'Benedicite,
Ye foul ball, whither will ye flee?'

And then, the seventeenth-century moralist, some 'seraphical' divine of King Charles II days, speaking of the vanity of human pursuits and occupations:

So have I seen the sun break forth from the cloudy dungeons of the night and climb high in the heavens, giving gladness to the hearts of men and gently unfolding the blossom of a rose, and affording light for all our toils and salutary labours and exemplary endeavours, that we be justified, if it be but a little, before the evening cometh, and the dull curtain of dark-

ness shut in all our scene, and it is time for a
reckoning and strict account of all that we have
performed. And yet within this brief allotted
space of salvation which may be the last
accorded to anyone, his life concluding with the
day, and sinking into the gloomy retirements
of the grave; yet have I seen men go forth in
their madness and unthriftiness, and waste the
hours of grace and of the sun, rendering to idle-
ness and wantonness and vain sport and pleasure the sum of all they owe to God and to man.
For such proceed to the places of their fond
diversion, and chase a painted bird with a
painted ball, till the sun vanishes under the
cloud of the night, and darkness encompasses
all things and the game is ended, and they have
their pains for their labours, and the remorse of
runagates for their choicest cogitations, and the
babble of fools in their ears in place of the
comfortable whisper of the angels as they lay
them down to rest and to that sleep which is
the quotidian prophecy of the tomb.

And so, at about the same period, Davenant
doggerelizes over the game in a different spirit:

But Husband grey now comes to stall,
For Prentice notch'd he strait does call;

Where's Dame, quoth he — quoth son of shop,
She's gone her cake in milk to sop:
Ho!   Ho! to Islington; enough!
Fetch Job my son and hearty stuff.
For there in sport we'll shout for luck,
And cry hay duck, there Dog, hay Duck.

And in the old song-books of ninety and a hundred years ago you may still occasionally come across —

THE TROLLERS' CATCH.

Trowl the ball slowly,
    So it pass wholly
The mark where the Duck would catch 'em;
    Thus shall it go
    Both sure and slow,
And that's the way to match 'em.
        Trollollilollilo.

And finally, Dog and Duck makes an odd casual appearance in one of the most remarkable trials of the eighteenth century, the famous case in which Anthony Mullins, citizen and haberdasher, was accused of the wilful murder of Thomas Jenkyns, a retired merchant, living at Enfield Wash. The body of Thomas Jenkyns was found in a pool of blood in a lonely field near Highbury; his throat being cut from ear to ear and, as one of the men who found the body declared: 'We were hard put to it to know what to do, for it seemed as if the poor man's head was almost cut away from his body, and I said to my friend, Richard Staple, who was with me: "Why, Dick," said I, "this is a villainous to-do; for if we make shift to raise the body 'tis a great chance that the man's head will fall apart, and I cannot abide the thought of it." "Why, Tom," says he, "I am much of your mind in the business. What if we leave ill work as it lies and go peaceably home by another way?" But I would not have that neither, lest, as I said, we should both be nabbed for the fact and come to Deadly Nevergreen (Tyburn) at last. And so we made shift to raise the dead man tenderly, I holding his head to his shoulders and trembling a great deal, and in this way brought him as far as Islington without any misadventure, it being late of a dark night without a moon and scarce anyone abroad.'

This murder, naturally enough, became the town talk of the day, the murdered man having many good friends in the city, and being both

wealthy and hospitable. It may be mentioned
by the way that the business of Mr. Thomas
Brown and Mr. Richard Staple, the two men
who found the body on that dark moonless
night, was more than dubious, and it was
conjectured that if the author of *Tom Jones*
had been still alive, he could have furnished
some interesting particulars as to their antece-
dents. However, no one suspected them of the
actual murder, since the dead man's watch was
on his body and ten guineas were found in his
purse, and that was a good defence, so far as
Tom and Dick were concerned. But there was
a great buzz of rumour everywhere, and more
especially in the northern parts of London, and
all the taverns were full of strange talk and
whispers of those who could tell strange tales,
and at last, at the end of the week, Anthony
Mullins was arrested and charged with the
murder, on the evidence of three persons who
swore that they had seen Mullins and the
murdered man together on the afternoon of
the day on which the crime was committed.

The three witnesses were: Simon Murchison,
a Scot, who kept a snuffshop in Norton Fol-
gate; William Frost, a brassfounder, of Clerken-
well; and Abraham Lewis, a clockmaker of

Devizes. These three persons, it appeared, met at the Bowl and Sword tavern in Islington, not having been previously acquainted with one another, and, warming over their cups, struck up an acquaintance, and spoke, as they declared, of ill trade and the decay of good old customs and the insolence of apprentices — they were all men in late middle age.

'We all grew to be pretty dismal over the bad times,' said Abraham Lewis in his evidence, 'till at last I said: "Why, neighbours, this will never end it or mend it. Come! let us go and bump it at Dog and Duck, and I will be surety for the first bowl of punch, the lowest score of the three to be debtor for the second." And so we went out into the alley behind the tavern, and Mr. Murchison ordered pipes and a plate of tobacco, and Mr. Frost bade the drawer bring brandy to hearten the bowl, and so we set to. Mr. Frost played the game very well and crossed the Duck three times and won the match, and I was second, so it fell to Mr. Murchison to call for the second bowl. And while we were in the arbour at the side of the alley, drinking our punch and smoking tobacco, and talking of the game, two men came out of the back door of the tavern and sat on a bench by the wall, speaking together very seriously, but not as we could hear what they said. They called for liquor, and drank two glasses apiece, and so went out, and we saw no more of them.'

And the witness swore that of these two men one was Mullins, the prisoner at the bar, and the other Jenkyns, the murdered man.

'I know him,' said Lewis, pointing to Mullins, 'by his great beaked nose, and the dead man I could swear to any day, for as he lifted his glass I saw that his little finger was crooked back, as if it had been broken; and I saw the body, and the little finger was crooked as I saw it on the live man.'

Lewis's evidence was corroborated in all essential details by his two tavern acquaintances. Murchison had noted that the prisoner had coughed, 'in a soft sort of fashion,' three or four times in the middle of his talk, and everybody in court had observed this peculiarity in Mullins as he stood in the dock. Frost described how he had seen the prisoner read a paper which the dead man had given him, and how Mullins had drawn out a very rich gold and tortoise-shell spectacle-case from his pocket, and had put on his spectacles to read the paper, and just such a spectacle-case, of an

uncommon pattern, was found on Mullins,
when he was arrested. And then Nancy Wilcox,
who was making merry with some gay friends
on ale and cheese-cakes at one of the Islington
taverns on the way to Highbury Fields, feeling,
as she said, a little heavy and stifled with the
heat of the place and the number of the company, went out to take the air and stood by the
tavern door. And Nancy swore that she saw the
prisoner pass close beside her, walking with
another man towards Highbury, but she would
not swear that the other man was Jenkyns,
though she vowed he was much like him.

Those in the court, barristers and spectators
alike, were confident that the noose was already
tight about Mullins' neck, when the great surprise of the trial startled them all. The prisoner's two clerks, Osborne and Nichols, swore
that their master had been with them the whole
afternoon, from three o'clock till eight in the
evening. And as the evidence of the three men
who played Dog and Duck and drank punch,
showed that they were at the 'Crown and Bowl'
tavern between three and five, while Nancy
Wilcox fixed her coming out to take the air as
'just a little after the clock had struck four; for
I said out loud, "There goes the stroke of four,

and there go four cups of ale too many,"'
it became of the utmost importance to the
Crown to shake the evidence of Osborne and
Nichols.

Osborne, it was explained, sat at a high desk
directly facing Mr. Mullins' private counting-
house, where he sat apart, in a place glazed in.
Nichols' desk was under a window, and looked
the other way, towards the door.

'I was busy with a great account,' said Osborne in court, 'but ever and again I looked up
from my book, and there sat my master as he
was always accustomed, but very still.'

COUNSEL. 'Was he not used, then, to sitting
still in the counting-house?'

OSBORNE. 'Why, not so. He would rise
now and again commonly and walk a little to
and fro, and so sit down again. And twice or
thrice in an hour he would come out and
speak with us about the occasions of the day.'

COUNSEL. 'And did he not stir at all on this
afternoon?'

OSBORNE. 'He sat still at his desk and never
moved till it was past eight in the evening.'

COUNSEL. 'And what did he then?'

OSBORNE. 'Why, he came forth with a very
slow step as if he were weary, and stood awhile

in the midst of the counting-house gazing about
him. And so, looking about him, he saw that
Nichols' place was empty, and he spoke to me
in a very sunken voice, little louder than a whisper, and said to me: "Where, then, is thy fellow?" Now the truth was that Mr. Nichols had
come softly to me where I sat with a candle on
my desk, for it began to grow dark, and he said
to me, speaking low: "Alas! my heart is very
heavy. I know not what it may be, but I am
sadly oppressed." I perceived that he shook a
great deal as he spoke, and his face was of a
pale colour, he being a ruddy man of his habit.
So to cheer him, I spoke hearty, but not loud,
and said, "Why, Jack, what's this? Never be
downhearted. Go you softly to the 'Mitre'
and drink a cup of ale and so defy the devil
and the dumps." Whereon he looked fear-
fully to the place where Mr. Mullins sat, with
no candle by him, and so crept out. Then, a
little while after, when my master came forth
and spoke as I have told it, I gave him the
truth, that Jack had the black dog on his
shoulders and I had counselled him to go out
to the "Mitre" and drink some ale to warm
his stomach and raise his spirits. "Alas!" said
Mr. Mullins, "poor child! He might do worse

than drink a cup of ale." And then came Nichols, and we two went away.'

Counsel. 'Did not the prisoner at the bar speak more with either of you?'

Osborne. 'No word more, but nodded his head as we went out.'

Counsel. 'And what did you then?'

Osborne. 'Why, I made such haste as I could away, for I was appointed to meet with one at Marylebone Gardens to view the fireworks, and it was very late.'

Counsel. 'Did you then part from Nichols?'

Osborne. 'Aye, for he told me that there was a supper of tripe waiting for him at his lodging by Pedlar's Acre an hour agone, and he feared lest all should be undone. "And so," quoth he, "since I won a wager of half a guinea but yesterday over the man that reads in the dark,[1] I'll e'en take water and begone with all speed." And so he fell to running very fast, and I saw him no more that night.'

[1] This must have been Jacob Courland, or Crowland, a foreigner. He had lost one eye in childhood, but possessed, as he declared, the power of seeing and reading in pitch darkness as well as in the brightest light. When in London he gave exhibitions of this singular faculty in a darkened room at the 'Sir Hugh Myddelton' tavern, Sadler's Wells, and afterwards at Salters' Hall.

All this was amply corroborated by Nichols. He was quite sure that Mullins had been in the counting-house all the afternoon, for, said he, 'My place was by the door, and I could not have failed to see him pass, if he had gone forth.' And then Counsel for the Crown, already hopeless of hanging the prisoner in the face of such evidence, asked him at hazard, what had been amiss with him on the afternoon of the murder. 'Are such fits common with you?' asked the Serjeant. 'You have the countenance of a hearty man.'

'Why, please you, so I am,' answered Nichols; 'and Hockley-in-the-Hole can answer for it. But on this afternoon there came quite suddenly a great trembling upon me, and a dread on my heart and a sickness in my stomach, and I did not know what ailed me, and I feared very much. And so I looked round on my stool, to see if my fellow, Osborne, was in his place, and looking down on the floor of the counting-house, I could have sworn that there was a great pool of blood there, with bubbles of blood in it, and I had almost swooned away for fear.'

Serjeant Munsey asked the witness no more questions, thinking him an idiot most likely, and the jury presently returned a verdict of 'not guilty,' and the prisoner, Mullins, was discharged.

There were rumours of an old and very bitter enmity between the murdered man and Mullins; but in face of the evidence of the two clerks that was nothing to the purpose. The murder of Thomas Jenkyns remains to this day as profound a mystery as the Campden Wonder — and that, after all, may be one of the inventions of Daniel Defoe.

Of late years, it is true, our occultists have been investigating the case from their peculiar viewpoint, and are satisfied, as far as I can make out, that Anthony Mullins was in two places at once. While the natural body of Anthony was engaged in committing murder at Highbury, his 'astral body' — whatever that may be — sat, or appeared to sit, in the accustomed chair in the counting-house. Possibly; but my own opinion is that the two clerks, Osborne and Nichols, perjured themselves to save their master, to whom, it afterwards appeared, they were much attached.

WHY NEW YEAR?

*

WHEN I was a boy, which is a good many years
ago, there was a very queer celebration on New
Year's Day in the little Monmouthshire town
where I was born, Caerleon-on-Usk. The town
children — village children would be nearer the
mark since the population of the place amounted
to a thousand souls or thereabouts — got the
biggest and bravest and gayest apple they could
find in the loft, deep in the dry bracken. They
put bits of gold leaf upon it. They stuck raisins
into it. They inserted into the apple little sprigs
of box, and then they delicately slit the ends of
hazel nuts, and so worked that the nuts appeared to grow from the ends of the box-
leaves, to be the disproportionate fruit of these
small trees. At last, three bits of stick were fixed
into the base of the apple, tripod-wise; and so
it was borne round from house to house; and the
children got cakes and sweets, and — those were
wild days, remember — small cups of ale. And
nobody knew what it was all about.

And here is the strangeness of it. Caerleon
means the fort of the legions, and for about three
hundred years the Second Augustan Legion

was quartered there, and made a tiny Rome of the place, with amphitheatre, baths, temples, and everything necessary for the comfort of a Roman-Briton. And the Legion brought over the custom of the *strena* (French, *étrennes*), the New Year's gift of good omen. The apple, with its gold leaf, raisins and nuts, meant: 'good crops and wealth in the New Year.' It is the Latin poet, Martial, I think, who alludes to the custom. He was an ungrateful fellow; somebody sent him a gold cup as a New Year's gift, and he said that the gold of the cup was so thin that it would have done very well to put on the festive apple of the day.

Well, I suppose the Second Augustan was recalled somewhere about A.D. 400. The Saxon came to Caerleon, and after him the Dane, and then the Norman, and then the modern spirit, the worst enemy of all, and still, up to fifty years ago, the Caerleon children kept New Year's Day, as if the Legionaries were yet in garrison. And I suppose that Caerleon was the only place south of the Tweed where people took any festal notice at all of the first day in the year. For it is not an old English festival at all. It is distinctly Latin in origin. The Latin peoples have always feasted the day; socially, it ranks far above Christmas in France. Where then do we get it? The answer is that we get it from the country where the whisky comes from. It is a Scottish feast. The Scots call it Hogmanay — a word that comes from an old song with the Latin burden, *hoc in anno*, 'in this year' — and the Scots who dwell amongst us have so popularized the celebration that it flourishes in England, so that we fancy it an old English custom. And the reason why the Scots keep New Year's Eve and New Year's Day with all the solemnities of whisky and good resolutions and elbow-joining and Auld-lang-syneing is that for many hundred years Scotland maintained the closest relations with France. Even to this day, I suppose, there are many Scots who would speak of table-linen as 'napery,' a cup as a 'tassie,' a leg of mutton as a 'gigot,' and a wild cherry as a 'gean.' In France, the *guigne* is a fruit half-way between the ordinary cherry and the morella, neither as sweet as the one nor as 'dry' as the other. France, indeed, has left all manner of trace on Scottish life. A small country town in Scotland reminds the travelled Englishman strangely of many a dull little town which he has visited in France; the sort of town which the French themselves call

29

'*un petit trou de province.*' The small Scots
town is not a bit like the small English town;
it lacks utterly the smugness, the warm, red
brick, comfortable appearance that one finds in
such places as Amersham, in Buckinghamshire,
Brandon, in Norfolk – or Suffolk? – and Marl-
borough, in Wiltshire. The county town of
Scotland is French, with a certain northern grim
ness about it, and if there is an old castle any-
where near, it will have the French *tourelles*, or
'pepperpot' turrets. And the cakes in the con-
fectioner's shop might be matched in France,
but hardly in Bond Street, for their choice
elaboration, their appeal, not only to the palate,
but the eye. And then the cooking: your lodging
may be of the humblest, but your landlady will
serve you such dishes in the way of Scots Broth
and Collops as you may pray for vainly all
England over. And after you have finished
your broth, the meat which made it will appear
on the table, garnished with its attendant herbs
and vegetables; just as in France, in many
country houses, the *bouilli*, the beef that made
the soup, is served after the soup plates have
been taken away.

Scotland, then, is largely a land of French
custom, and thus, ultimately, of Roman cus-

tom. The Scots Law is largely Roman Law. They have no coroner in Scotland. The Procurator Fiscal 'precognoses' the case as the Procureur de la République makes his 'instruction,' his preliminary inquiry in France. And so, Scotland has given us her Latin-French festival of New Year's Day. And it has 'caught on' wonderfully. Not, I think, quite in the true spirit of its native lands, Rome and France and Scotland. I spoke of 'good resolutions' as part of the New Year ritual; but that, perhaps, is our grave English contribution to the feast. We speak of a 'Merry Christmas and a Happy New Year,' and I believe that no Englishman is quite all mirth as the clock begins to strike midnight on December 31st. He may wish to be purely jolly; but somehow a tinge of solemnity will break in on his jollity. There will never be quite the abandonment of Christmas in our New Year's mirth. We may be as worldly as we will; but in the last five minutes before the bell of twelve, I believe that a little of the Watch Night spirit of the Methodists finds its way into the cups and strikes a silence about the board.

ON VALENTINES AND OTHER
THINGS

★

IT is a theory of mine that one very rarely sees the last of anything. In a sense, of course, we have seen the last of the horsed omnibuses of London; we know that we shall never more behold them lumbering along the streets; those vehicles that would look almost like toys to us now, but then seemed great and gay. The last one that I saw at all was quiescent, and not in motion. There is a wharf by the canal somewhere in Camden Town. It looks as if somebody had thought of pulling it down or of turning it into something else, and had then despaired of his endeavour. On this wharf I noted, a few years ago, an old omnibus standing desolate. It is possible that the owner of the wharf had a notion that it would make a good barge: but this fancy also went the way of his other dreams. We have seen the last of the horse-omnibuses in one sense, but who can come forward and declare that he was a passenger in or on the last journey made by the last horse-omnibus in London? The old machine endured, I think, into the war. I tried to keep my eye on one that plied from Somerset House to Waterloo and back; but it faded imperceptibly and was gone. So with the Valentine. Who bought the last Valentine, and when? I can remember very well indeed the days in which the fourteenth of the month of February came with a flutter of excitement to the breakfast-table. There was no knowing what the post might or might not bring in the way of sentiment or comedy. There were the fine and scented Valentines in cardboard boxes, puffy with cotton-wool and the tenderest feelings; things of silk and satin, delicately scented, painted with flowers. And then there was satire of the milder kind, pictures of absurd young men holding crutchsticks and chewing toothpicks and looking foolish. These mortified the more sensitive recipients; and there was always the anxiety of wondering whose hand had sped the dart. The writing on the envelope was of course disguised, or written by some person whose script was unknown to the receiver of the Valentine. Hence the question: was it only that fool Bill; or, alas! was it from the fair adored Hermione?

But there was a third class of Valentine; the kind which the butcher's boy sent to the cook, which the housemaid dispatched to the young greengrocer whose suit she scorned. No 'nice' stationer kept these Valentines. They were to be sought in back streets, near the rag-and-bone shop, close at hand to the broken-down furniture warehouse. They stood in rows in the windows of mean shops; things made of the thinnest paper, about five inches broad by eighteen long. They bore hideous libels on the human form, outlined in black with liberal splashes of coarse red paint, usually determining to the nose. On these things cook, who in real life was a pleasant, comfortable body, would find herself depicted as bloated beyond recognition. Beside her a bottle of brandy, half finished, might stand, and a horrid verse below would sing:

You always find the kitchen dripping handy:
You know the way to turn it into brandy.

Thus insinuating against the poor woman the vice, not only of dishonesty, but inebriety. So the young greengrocer would be counselled to keep his carrots for his own consumption, instead of wasting them on his ass:

To say the least,
If he's a four-legged, you're a two-legged beast.

And so on, and so on. The satire was somewhat ponderous, perhaps; but those were hearty days. The butcher boy, in particular, was an irresistible and an easy mark. Here was the opportunity for the red pigment, and plenty of it. The poor lad was depicted as gnawing a huge and bloody bone with loathsome appetite and hideous grimaces, and underneath would run the legend:

> You starved so long at home
> You went abroad to gnaw a bone.

And all these fine, brave things are gone! It is years upon years since I have seen them hung up in the small shops in the back streets. I think, somehow, that the last of all must have been on view in the purlieus of Hoxton; Hoxton the home of lost causes; the last place to have a genuine theatrical stock company, the last place, I fear, which will make the toy theatre, the delight of so many childhoods that have since turned to dismal old age. And I am wondering whether any collector, wise in time, felt by instinct that the day of the vulgar Valentines was almost done, and so collected them forthwith. Probably such a man arose in the nick of time; a man who specialized in this one subject, and could tell you the very year of the first Valentine depicting that bloated cook and that sanguineous butcher boy, of the firm which had the monopoly of their production. If you know this man he will show you his portfolio of back-street Valentines, and point out the rarer specimens, even the unique Undertaker Valentine, a lachrymose and drunken fellow, shedding hypocritical tears, and illustrating the couplet:

You swab your eyes, but not with grief,
You want more gin for your relief.

There must be some such collection, I am sure, and if it is but given time to age, it will become valuable. For here is one of the most curious things in that complex which we call human nature; age will give merit to anything, or almost anything. The vulgarest abuse scrawled on the walls of Pompeii has a huge interest to us; and the time will come when those old pasquinades of the London slums of twenty, thirty, fifty years ago may give more delight than grave books full of science. For, if one thinks it over, it will appear that science, which has always assumed such great airs, is one of the most fleeting and evanescent of things. It does not last; it becomes perilously near nothing at all. Take a chemistry book of twenty-five years ago, with its dogmas of the intransmutable elements, and the atom as the ultimate of matter. The elements, or some of them, have been transmuted; the atom is a universe of electrons: the chemistry of 1895 is but an idle tale. But old fellows will still chuckle as they draw their bald old heads together in the club window and recall the remark made by the driver of the 'John Bull' to the conductor of the yellow 'Tilling' in 1895, one fine summer evening.

I think some substitute should be found for the vanished Valentine and its observances. Suppose we made February 14 a day on which we could do what we liked – of course without malice or injury to our neighbours. Suppose we made a regular wild day of it, and insisted on buying chocolate creams – and why not bullseyes? – at 8.15 p.m.; on having another glass of small beer after ten, on buying cigarettes openly at eleven.

Why not – to use a vulgar old expression – go the whole hog on St. Valentine's Day, and make believe we are Englishmen again, not inmates of a Home of Care and Restraint for the Feeble-minded?

'MOTHERING Sunday,' we may take it, falls, in ninety-nine cases out of a hundred, in the month of March. I should not like to be too precise, since the calculation of the date of Easter is a very knotty matter, and the oldest difference to divide Christendom into two camps. Moreover, I have not got the Dominical Letter, the Golden Number and the Epact by me; and you must have all these handy if you would talk about Easter and the dates dependent on it. But, on the whole, I think we may say safely that Mothering Sunday – called also Mi-Carême, Mid-Lent, and Refreshment Sunday – falls in March. We will not go into the question of the origin of the name 'Mothering' – a very pleasant, friendly and homely title. There are certain words in the Epistle for the day which may account for it; at all events, this Sunday has always been celebrated as a feast in the midst of a fast. And I have a very vivid recollection of the manner in which the festival was observed in the west country about fifty years ago. I was not very old then; and the ritual appealed to me highly. I can well remember the aspect of the country town on the Saturday, the market day, before Mothering Sunday. Or, I should say, the aspect of the confectioners' shops in the narrow high street. For they were more gorgeous on this day than on the market day before Christmas. They were full of cakes, cakes for every purse, wonderfully adorned with icing, white and pink; a truly delicious spectacle. For the custom of the country was that on the day following, Mothering Sunday, every child should present his mother with a cake. I believe that farm-servants, in especial, made a great point of this observance. Out of slender savings — five or six or seven pounds a year were their wages in those days — they would buy a cake and beg leave of absence from the farmer on the Sunday, tramping, some of them, ten miles over the hills to the maternal cottage, there to make their offering, and warm their hands at the old hearth before setting out again for the farm by deep lanes and black March woods. A friendly, kindly custom; one of the good observances that smoothed the rough places of life in the old days.

Now these kind cakes were, of course, Simnel cakes, though I do not recollect whether they were prepared according to the usual recipe which so pleasantly puts a layer of almond-paste not only outside the cake but in its very vitals. And, that everything should be pleasant about this mid-Lent festivity, some ingenious person was at the pains to invent an etymology for the word Simnel, which is matchless in its absurdity. Simnel was just mediæval English for a cake. It comes from the Latin, *Simila*, which means the finest wheaten flour. Originally, I suppose, the English word was 'simmel,' this became 'simnel' as 'pantomime' becomes – on some lips – 'pantomine.' But about eighty or a hundred years ago, the ingenious person got to work on simnel. I conjecture that he had settled that Charing was, really, *chère reine*; a touching allusion to Queen Eleanor. He had shrunk from the vulgarity of Rotten Row and had demonstrated that it was a corruption of *Route du Roi*. He had made Birdcage Walk into Bocage Walk, and had explained how energetic apprentices sometimes set the *tems*, or sieve, on fire. Refreshed by these labours he turned his eye on simnel – and produced his masterpiece.

Once on a time, it appears, there was an old

couple, Sim and Nell by name. They were dear old people, with the best hearts in the world, but after many long years of happy married life, they had retained their several individualities. And so, when it came to a question of their having a cake, there was something of a dispute. One — I forget which — wanted it baked; the other would have a cake that was boiled. So, one regrets to say it, they differed and even quarrelled as to this cake; the debate rose to such a pitch that Nell rushed at Sim with the broom. In her violence, she broke some eggs that lay on the table, and this catastrophe brought these nice old people to their senses. They saw that they had been silly. They agreed that, to please both parties, the famous cake should be part baked, part boiled. And to round off all, and to smooth everything over, literally and meta-phorically, the smashed eggs should be used to glaze the cake. And so, from this quarrel and reconciliation between Sim and Nell, the cake was naturally called Sim-nel.

There; that is the etymology; and in the words of my favourite classic, 'Get Rich Quick Wallingford': 'Can Limburger smell worse?' But I confess to being curious as to the iden-

tity of the inventor of this ridiculous and
imbecile fable. Was he one with the inventor
of the other etymologies which I have mentioned, or was he 'a little syndicate,' operating
in false derivations? — I forgot, by the way, one
of the noblest efforts in this kind: the account
of how the tavern sign of 'The Goat and
Compasses' arose from the piety of Puritan
days, when the Sour Saints drank their ale
under the proclamation, 'God Encompasseth
Us.' But, as I say, the mental process of the
individual, or individuals, who invented the
simnel nonsense, and all the other like non-
senses, interests me. Was he a leg-puller, who
deliberately made up idiotic tales, chuckling
as he reflected that there was no limit to human
folly? Or was he merely a solemn ignoramus,
with a misdirected zeal for piercing to the
root of things, who sat down, as it were, before
any word or phrase that he did not under-
stand, and set his weak brains working until
they evolved a feeble fable? It will ever be a
mystery. In all probability, the person who
invented these outrageous tales was a Rationalist, a man with the scientific mind. He
perceived that it was all nonsense to talk of
setting the Thames on fire; the thing couldn't

be done. He didn't know that every nation has the proverb, the name of the river being varied. So he made up his ingenious story of the energetic apprentice and his sieve, or whatever the *tems* may be. And so again; never having heard of *simila*, fine, sifted flour, he made up the tragi-comedy of Sim and Nell.

'APRIL FOOL!'

*

Does the rite of the April fool still survive amongst us? Or has it gone the way of the February Valentine and of the ceremony of the oak-apple on the twenty-ninth of May? I am afraid that if it has not gone it is going fast, like most of the light-hearted observances which our fathers loved.

I can remember the time when on the first of April men ordinarily grave and sedate enough would invent mad errands for the simple. Boys would be sent to the chemist's for a pint of pigeon's milk or to the cobbler's for a certain quantity of 'strap oil'; these April jests were mostly jokes of much the same quality as the actor's trick of sending the beginner to borrow an 'ibid,' a mysterious prop. which had its origin in the list of characters and their costumes at the beginning of the old play books. Thus, the Duke of Otranto — let us say — was to wear a black velvet mantle, black hose and shoes, and a cap with a black plume in the first act. Then, for the second act, he would be set down 'ibid'; that is, *ibidem;* stage Latin for 'same costume.' The young actor would go forth on his search for the ibid, and be sent from the vaults underneath the stage to the flies, and climb many stairs and peer into many strange dens before he became convinced that he might as well look for an ibis as an ibid; and such was the spirit of the ceremony and quest of the April fool. The whole principle of the business was that you were to send somebody to look for something that didn't exist and moreover wasn't there! Thus, it would be very graceful April Foolery if I were to have a number of cards printed reading like this:

HAMPTON COURT

THE FIRST COMMISSIONER OF WORKS
Requests the honour of your company
AT THE FEEDING OF THE DRAGONS

April 1st.
Eleven o'clock precisely.
Morning dress.

And as I write this nonsense, the conviction seizes me that every hundred such cards sent out would find at least five April fools, and very likely more. The older I grow, the more firmly

I am convinced that there is no proposition, tale or statement so monstrous that it will not find some true believers. I feel certain that if I announced an Exhibition of Two-Sided Triangles, I should have numerous inquiries; and I think I could find modern artists who would paint them for me. No proposition is too absurd for belief; I knew hard-headed men of business who grew cross and heated if you hinted some doubt as to those tens of thousands of Russian soldiers who had passed through Ealing Broadway 'last Sunday morning, between ten and eleven; my brother saw them, I tell you.' Why, it is only a few weeks since I saw an odd-looking picture on the back page of a newspaper. It was, like the rest of the pictures on the page, a reproduction of a photograph. Most of it was ordinary enough; it showed a girl standing against a background of leafage. But close to the girl's head there was something not so ordinary; a little winged figure, perhaps six inches long, clothed in some gauzy stuff, appearing to float in the air, in the manner of a butterfly. That little winged figure was a fairy!

This 'fairy' is believed in and commented on by grave men, men of undoubted culture, men of undoubted intelligence – in other matters, at all events. Nay, serious scientific language is brought in to explain these *in camera* fairies: they are invisible to most mortal eyes, it appears, but the ultra-violet rays perceive them and fix them on the photographic plate. And their intelligence is measured by the experts; it is equal to that of the average Newfoundland dog, or perhaps a little lower. And their business? Skilled and scientific, they build up the molecules which compose the flowers.

There you are! I believe I should have a mob waiting to see the Hampton Court Dragons fed — if I placed my cards with a certain discretion.

And another instance. A dozen years ago or so, an old friend of mine, a musician, was in the artists' room of a provincial concert hall. A concert was going on, and my friend's attention was attracted by the sound of a certain showy but indifferent piece of modern violin music from the platform.

'What are they playing that thing for?' he asked somewhat contemptuously of another artist, a lady who was standing by him.

'Oh, didn't you hear,' she replied, in a sort of reverent church whisper; 'the Holy Grail ordered it to be played.'

The monstrous April Fool story on which this remark hung is much too long to be told here in its full significance. But briefly: somebody a few years ago picked up in a French curiosity-shop a queer saucer-like vessel of blue glass. Somebody else, seeing the thing, remarked: 'I always think the Holy Grail must have been like that'; and so, by certain elaborate stages, the saucer — a modern imitation of antique glass, said the antiquaries — became the Holy Grail, gave oracles, diffused blessedness, and meddled with concert programmes.

'This way for the Dragons, ladies and gentlemen!'

And now, as the preacher says, for the application. It seems pretty clear, I think, from these examples, that some of us are April Fools all the year round. There is no tale too outrageous for us to swallow, no quest too absurd for us to undertake. Pigeons' milk, indeed! We are ready to fetch quarts of it, gallons. And it is possible that the wise men of old, from whom all good customs and strange ceremonies proceed, perceived this abounding folly of the human heart, and devised the rite of the April fool, that thereby we might be purged of absurd credulity by 'pity and terror,' as Aristotle has it. 'Let there be an orgie of folly on one day in the year,' these sages may have said, 'so that thereby it may exhaust itself, and learn its own mad excess, and refrain itself for the remaining three hundred and sixty-four days.' There is, of course, another explanation, known to a few. According to these people, the April Fool business is, like many other popular customs, games, and ceremonies, the remnant of a rite or mystery of the most profound antiquity. This rite, as it is declared, instructed those who had 'passed the doors' that most of the business of the world, especially that business commonly regarded as most weighty, important, grave and serious, is a crazy quest, a search for what doesn't exist and isn't there. So, say these authorities, the initiated were instructed that most of the reputed great, serious, portentous and weighty men of this world, on arriving in the other world, will be received with undying shouts of mirth and by a voice pealing in an unknown tongue a pretty close equivalent to 'April Fool!'

I HAVE been reading about the customs of May
Day; of the rising up early and going into the
fields and to the borders of the woods, of the
gathering of the white blossoming boughs and
the bearing of them home again. And of the
Maypole also; of the tall tree all bedecked and
garlanded and gay; and the men and women
dancing round it, in sheer lightness of heart, in
sheer delight that the sun is warm once more,
and that the earth once more has grown green.
I wonder and admire and am quite sure that the
age which performed all these happy observances was, so far, infinitely more civilized than
ours, which, I believe, observes May Day, so far
as it observes the feast at all, by holding demon-
strations of a scarlet colour and holloing of Bolshevist anthems. Without going deeply into
politics, one can say quite definitely that it is
more civilized to bear branches of flowering
thorn than to bear the Red Flag. But, having
freely admitted this much, I would urge my
strong objection to the attempted revival of May
Day customs – or of any old customs for the
matter of that. What is the use of tying grapes

on thorns or figs on thistles? You may make a ghastly and unconvincing imitation of a vine, and a fig, but the fruits will rot and the thorn will remain a thorn, and the thistle a thistle. It is without the slightest enthusiasm that I read of the revival of Morris dancing and the teaching of it; it is as if one taught laughter in the Council Schools. Little pamphlets and magazine articles would be written showing how our old English literature is full of allusions to mirth and laughter, how once upon a time everybody laughed, how an old man had been found in an out-of-the-way hamlet who still laughed, how many eminent physiologists were inclined to think that laughter, in some mysterious manner, promoted digestion. You can imagine the scene: the schoolroom smelling of damp deal boards and inkpots, its walls hung round with maps and charts, the mistress — certificated in Laughter — at her desk.

'Now, children,' she begins, 'I have explained to you how once upon a time everybody laughed a great deal. We don't quite know why they did so. Some learned men think that laughter was an imitation of a thunderstorm, and that people laughed to bring the thunder and rain and do good to the crops, just as sailors used to whistle when they wanted the wind to blow and make their ship go through the water. You heard all about that the other day in Miss Skimpton's lecture on the Mimetic and Cultural Origin of the Arts. But, whatever the reason for people laughing, it is thought that it was good for them and that it would be good for us too.

'Now, children, imitate me –'

THE MISTRESS – *sadly* – 'Ha, ha, ha!'

THE CHILDREN – *gloomily* – 'Ha, ha, ha!'

THE MISTRESS – *miserably* – 'He, he, he!'

THE CHILDREN – *despairingly* – 'He, he, he!'

Well, it may come to that, if the world goes on as it goes now, and laughter may become a lost art. But it will be of no use to try to 'revive' it. It will be idle to put it into a syllabus and teach it in the schools. And so it is idle and useless to try to revive Morris dancing or May games or Maypoles or any of the ancient customs of our fathers. For these things are effects, symptoms; not causes. You cannot get scarlet fever by painting yourself with red spots; you cannot get a light and happy heart by dancing a Morris or dancing round the Maypole or bringing in the May. The German baron in the story was found jumping over his chairs and tables. He was asked what he meant by it, and he replied: 'Sh'apprens t'être fif' – by which he intended to say: 'I am learning to be lively.' But it is quite certain that he remained as heavy as ever. And it is quite certain that we have lost that quality which lay behind all these old merry customs of the May, which was the cause and source of them all. I have called that quality light-heartedness, but I am not sure but that joy is not the real name. It is already becoming something of a mystery to us, as the origin and cause and meaning of laughter had become to our imaginary County Council mistress. It was not a thing that depended upon external good fortune or ill; people had hard times and bad luck in plenty in the Middle Ages, and bad luck of a very ill kind: we may be sure of that. But, as a race, we always had joy, and that in an eminent degree, as is expressed by the phrase, 'Merry England.' We must not confuse this sense of mirth or joy or light-heartedness – whatever it may be called – with the sense of humour. *That*, I think, we have in a superior degree; all of us, that is, who can relish Dickens and W. W. Jacobs. The mediæval notion of a joke was primitive and practical; there are certain tales in Chaucer which are assuredly funny, but in a rough and ready way, and without the subtler flavours which we have learned to relish and appreciate. But humour has nothing much to do with a light heart; its savour is not far removed from sadness. Humour, we may almost say, is a strange and beautiful and exquisite by-product of a world which is seen to be all wrong; a recognition that its incoherences and even its tragedies have something wildly funny about them. Let us review Mr. Micawber's career as it appeared to the eyes of the world and Mrs. Micawber's family; it was, seriously, rather shocking, disastrous, and not over honest. I don't think the Middle Ages would have seen anything funny in Micawber: they would probably have whippd him. But Dickens, by a happy and marvellous magic, distilled Micawber's shabby disgraces into an elixir of rare humour.

But that quality which we have been speaking of, that quality which made Morris dances and May mirth, which caused grave lawyers to dance solemnly round an imaginary fireplace in Middle Temple Hall as late as the beginning of the eighteenth century — that quality was due to a conviction that in spite of the Black Death and the Hangman and the King's Counsellors the times were on the whole in joint, and not out of joint. Dante wrote of horrors terrible enough, and many of them eternal horrors; yet, surveying the universe, he could call his book, the 'Divine Comedy.' He could afford to be light-hearted. Not only the end, but the whole purpose and scheme, as he saw it, were happy. I think that this joy, this mirth, had departed from the world, or were fast departing from it, when Shakespeare wrote. His outlook on the universe was, I believe, on the whole, a sad one. It was thus that he was able to create Falstaff, that supreme work of humour out of the villainies and cowardices and shameful shifts of one of the most disgraceful old rascals who ever breathed in imaginative literature. To Chaucer, Falstaff would have been merely a 'recreant knight' and 'foul caitiff': but Shakespeare saw him as a fountain bubbling with laughter.

★

IT was in April, if I remember, that I said something about fairies. I am afraid I was talking about April fools, and more or less maintaining that they flourished not only in April but all the year round. And one example was the case of the Yorkshire Fairies, as we may conveniently call them. Or, if you like, we will be good journalists and call them the 'alleged' fairies. You know the story. Two young ladies of Yorkshire – one of them, I think, has had some practical and professional experience in the art of photography – were in the habit of taking country rambles and snapshots together. When the plates were developed, strange to say, besides the portrait and the leafage and the flowers there appeared certain forms which were easily recognizable as fairies – as the fairies of a somewhat third-rate artistic conception. Scaling the little figure against the girl's face, I should give the tiny being some nine or ten inches of height. It was draped. It had the familiar wings of the fairies in all the pictures in all the children's fairy-tale books. If you were producing a fairy play for Christmas you would dress your chorus exactly as the photographic fairy is dressed; and the 'principals' would wear a similar, though richer, habit and have like wings, more brilliantly spangled. In a word, the fairy of the photographs is the conventional fairy and nothing else. And that is why I cannot believe in that fairy. For I cannot suppose that the modern inventions of nineteenth-century story-tellers, artists and stage managers can have projected themselves into nature; and no such fairies as these deal in have any place in ancient tradition. It is June; the month of the fairies, of the Midsummer Night's Dream; let us occupy ourselves a little with the fair people.

To begin with the conventional fairy, the fairy of the photograph, the fairy that we have been discussing. I trace this little creature back to Shakespeare and Herrick. Queen Mab in Mercutio's speech rode abroad in an empty hazel nut; Herrick's Oberon drinks his wine from a daisy, and his loaf is a grain of wheat. Here are minute entities, indeed. Queen Mab is to be conceived as of about the size of a house-fly; Oberon may be almost as huge as a harvest mouse. Hans Andersen, who dealt more in fancy than in folk-lore, has such fairies in some of his tales; fairies that he concealed in tulips.

But, so far as I know, this minute fairy is a purely literary invention. It is first met in Elizabethan literature; it puts on a few inches in the fairy tales of the nineteenth century, chiefly, I suppose, because a fairy queen no bigger than a fly is too small to be handled, either by writer or artist. The children's fairy-tale fairy becomes about the size of the Yorkshire photographic fairy; anything between six inches and a foot high. But, as I say, neither the minute Mab, the tiny Oberon of Herrick, nor the picture-book sprite of modern times has any original in true popular tradition. The fairies were, indeed, the 'Little People,' and hence, perhaps, the poets, exaggerating, thought of Mab small enough to ride in a hazel nut. But the older conception is also illustrated by Shakespeare. The sham fairies who plague Falstaff in 'The Merry Wives of Windsor' are impersonated by Windsor children. They are imagined, then, to be beings from three to four feet high; and such was the traditional height of the 'Little People.' Such is the figure of the Irish Leprechaun — the fairy cobbler with the pot of gold.

There is a very tempting theory which now comes in our way. It has been held that the tradition of the fairies is, in fact, the tradition preserved amongst the Celts of the small, dark race which they supplanted. There is a good deal to be said for this. It is only a few years ago that a certain hill in Ireland was excavated. This hill had been known from time immemorial and was still known as a Fairy Rath. The Little People dwelt within it; the light of their fires had been seen shining from it of dark nights.

And the queer thing is that this was perfectly true. Or rather, it had been true – a thousand years ago. For the exploration of the hill showed that the primitive pre-Celtic race had dwelt within it, till the Danes broke into their hiding-place somewhere in the tenth century. And the fairy lights? The blocked-up chimney shaft of the hidden house in the hill was disclosed. No doubt, when the Little People made great fires the flames shot up and flickered on the hill-top; and were seen by some trembling wandering man astray in the wilds and the darkness. What a tale that man told when he found his way at last to friendlier fires; with the door set fast! And the stories of the fair children taken away to live in the hollow hill by the Little People, of the dark, wizened babes, the changelings, left in their place? Likely enough these things happened.

It is probable, then, that the pre-Celtic inhabitants of these islands may account for a great deal of fairy tradition; but not, I think, for all. The fairies are also gods and goddesses of the old time now diminished in dignity but still potent; and, be it remarked, always, or almost always, evil. About forty years ago I was talking of old ways with an elderly Monmouthshire farmer, and he told me that in his youth people used to put the May blossom on the doorsteps of their houses – to keep the fairies out. So, when I was driving eight years ago in the country near Belfast, my friend, a hard-headed Presbyterian man of business, showed me the mountain-ash trees planted by every house – to keep the fairies out. We have come a long way from the fancies of Shakespeare and Herrick, a long way indeed from the benevolent little beings of the children's books. In true popular tradition the fairies are always dreaded; partly, perhaps, because they were old gods and goddesses, accursed by the Christian Faith, partly because they were the little dark people who lived in the hills and stole away the fair Celtic children from the Christian hearth. There, I think, you have the main strands in fairy tradition. But there are others. A fairy is sometimes an 'elemental,' a spirit of one of the four elements, according to the ancient theory of elements; air, fire, earth, water. The Sylphs were of the air, the Salamanders of the fire, the Gnomes of the earth, the Undines of the water; and I am sorry to say I do not know how far Paracelsus, who made this classification, was deriving from tradition and how far he was inventing or drawing on his reading in queer, forbidden manuscripts. And I am not clear as to the character of these spirits of the elements. Some servants' 'characters' are obscure, and so it is here. But I do not remember to have heard any particular good of Salamanders, considered, that is, as spirits of flame, and insinuating nothing against a harmless lizard of that name or against a cooking utensil which might be used more than it is. But on the elementals, read 'Le Comte de Gabalis,' a singular treatise of the seventeenth century.

Again, you have another kind of fairy; the Robin Goodfellow, Lob-lie-by-the-fire, the Lubber fiend; who would work hard for you at nights and thresh out your corn if you set a great bowl of cream for his refreshment. And last of all there is the Fairy Queen whom mortals sometimes visit, who, as in Walter Map's tale, makes three hundred years seem but the passing of a single night. Such was the lady to whom Thomas of Ercildoune returned at last. I am not sure whether she is the lady whom Tannhauser knew; the lady Venus; but I am certain that she has nothing to do with the Yorkshire fairy on the photographic plate.

JULY SPORT
WITH SOME REMARKS ON YOUNG MR. BLUEFACE

★

ONE July picture always remains clear in my mind. A heavy, sweltering heat, a dark sky with darker clouds moving across it, a promise of heavy rain – usually fulfilled – in the still air, a river flowing down from an ancient grey bridge between rich meadows, lawns and gardens and overhanging trees, vanishing beyond a wooded point beneath high leafy hills. Altogether, a beautiful English landscape, improved to my mind by the temple in eighteenth-century classic, which, if I remember, stands among the trees down stream; it is the Thames at Henley.

All the foreground of the river, on the town side, is full of boats, and the boats are full of pretty girls in pretty summery frocks talking to young men in blazers of every device with the arms of all colleges embroidered upon them. And the boats are gay with cushions of all colours, and queer entertainers wearing pink mortar-boards and blue coats and yellow trousers and black faces move up and down the river twanging the banjo and singing; altogether a very lively scene. Then, a gun is heard in the

63

distance by the point, and up come the boats. The men row for their lives – and it is not their fault that in these days of the motor they cannot give the notion of tremendous speed – and the race is decided somewhere opposite to the boats full of pretty girls and blazers.

Now, it has once or twice been my business to be on a stand just at this point, and I have therefore had the opportunity of observing what happens to the crews when the race is over. They do not look happy. Some of them fall backward. Some of them lurch forward, their heads between their knees. Some of them have open mouths, and they gasp for breath after the fashion of fish out of the water. Some of their faces are blue. And there can be no doubt that some of them will suffer from the effects of that boat race for the rest of their lives. And the puzzle of it is that all this is done for fun. They row because they like it; it is not one of the 'extraordinary punishments' which the seventeenth-century Puritans accused the Star Chamber of inflicting; it is no cruel sentence of an arbitrary and oppressive court that has condemned these young men to so many minutes of bodily torture. And let it be remembered that there has been a long period of chronic unpleasantness before the acute agony of the race. All these men have kept a kind of athletic Ramadan. They have gone into training. Their meats and their drinks have been regulated for them, their stomachs have been handed over to the trainer, every muscle of their bodies has been under strict inspection, they have had to rise at abominably early hours and go to sleep soon after the children are put to bed — and, worst of all, their tobacco has been cut off. In fact, these men in the boat have gladly consented to a rule sterner than that of a Benedictine monastery, all for the sake of this final ten minutes of long-pumping, heart-wracking, muscle-burning torment, called a boat race.

There it is; and all done voluntarily, nay, eagerly, for the pleasure, the delight of the thing. It may be said that these rowing men endure what they endure and suffer what they suffer in order that they may win. And, very likely, the men themselves think so; but they are mistaken. The winning of the race, which is, formally and in theory, the object and the reason of the whole thing, is in reality an after-thought, a cunning excuse. Excuse for what?

The priests of Baal, it may be remembered, cut themselves with knives after their manner.

They pretended that they behaved in this odd way because they wanted Baal to hear them, just as our young white-robed priests of the Holy Boat pretend they go through all the torments that have been described because they want to have absurd objects called Diamond Sculls and Golden Goblets in their nominal possession for the twelve ensuing months. Both sets of priests lie, as Dr. Johnson would say, or, as we should say, are mistaken. The priests of Baal cut themselves with knives because they liked cutting themselves with knives, and the priests of Henley subject themselves to almost intolerable distress because they enjoy doing so. And it won't do to say that they turn blue and gasp because of the honour and renown, because the pretty girls in the summery frocks love him that gaspeth, whose face is even of the colour of lead. Watch the after career of one of these men. Likely enough, you may see him in a photograph, a year or two later. The scene is an awful one. All about are hideous desolations of ice and snow. There are black gulfs as horrible as if they were prepared for Titans' graves. There are sheer depths that terrify even in a picture; precipices that your soul will remember in those dreams from which men awake sweating and shrieking. And high over these unutterable frozen wastes, high above four thousand feet of nothingness, a rock juts out precipitous. It is a smooth wall, and it leans, as it were, towards you as you look at the picture. On this sloping rock, stretched out like a spatch-cocked fowl, is young Blueface, late of Henley. He is holding on by teeth and feet and nails to fragments of uncertain stability; the failure of a quarter of an inch will send him plunging through those four thousand feet of empty air to destruction. If he is lucky, he will get to the top of that unpleasant rock and see a frightful landscape, not unlike the horrid lakes and mountains of the moon. He will then turn, and face the equal perils of the descent. And he does all this because he likes it; likes it even better than the induced suffocation and heart-disease at Henley.

And, this time, let it be noted, young Blueface has no admiring audience. There are no pretty, summery girls to be melted. There are no harmless drudges of the Press peering from their stand over the abyss, ready to record his achievement in double-leaded longprimer. There may be a paragraph in the 'Alpinist' — only seen by fellow-fakirs — mentioning briefly

Mr. Blueface's successful climb of the Dummer-kopf; or another sort of paragraph headed 'Alpine Fatality.' Blueface himself will never speak of the affair willingly. If you apply strong pressure to him you may squeeze out a sort of half-admission that 'the last lap of the old mound was a bit tricky'; and then he will change the subject and ask you if you have heard anything about Bolter and what you fancy for the Cantershire. Again; there it is. The terrors and the horrible dangers and the frightful bodily and mental strain of Alpine climbing are faced freely and voluntarily because they are enjoyed. Nay, take Mr. Blueface in his leisure moments, when he is resting from his acuter pleasures. It is a hot, a very hot afternoon. The thermometer mounts to 87. Existence is just bearable if you keep perfectly still. The logical understanding suggests a hammock or a deck chair in the deepest shade, a curiously compounded drink with ice, in a very long glass, and a placid pipe. What does young Blueface do? He finds another like unto him, and they get into the full blaze of the sun with a net between them, and proceed to hit a ball with a racket in the most violent manner, and to rush to and fro with tremendous speed for the next three hours, till they are as like burning coals as human beings may be.

Long ago a French book was written called *À quoi tient la Supériorité des Anglo-Saxones? What is the Secret of Anglo-Saxon Supremacy?* So far as I remember, the work in question offered no very helpful solution of the mystery; perhaps, we may venture to say that we owe a great deal to the fact that we have invented an odd ritual, called sport, which gives one of the most deep-seated instincts of humanity an opportunity of gratification.

*

Two happy, musty tags of quotation occur to me as I contemplate this month of August. One is the classic adage which informs you in a grave and ancient manner that you may fork out nature as many times as you like; but back she will come, again and again. The other tag is from the French: Change and change and change again; still the same it will remain. And putting the two together, you have the solution of the problem of the Londoner's holiday. Why is it that when he goes away for a change he looks out for some place that is as like London as possible?

You see? Expel nature with a fork; tell Mr. Londoner that what he wants is a thorough change, that he must be off to the sea-breezes and the sea-bathing of the peaceful little fishing village of Brighthelmstone, on the Sussex coast. In a very few years the Thrales have heard of it, and Jack Wilkes has heard of it, and the Prince has heard of it; and the peaceful little village of Brighthelmstone has become Brighton, a fashionable place, a place with smart shops and smart hotels, in a word, as good an imitation of

London as can be knocked up on the bit of coast under the Downs. You can certainly bathe if you like, and you cannot help breathing the good salt air; but the point is that Brighton is the Londoner's home from home. And so, to refer back to the second tag, the more he is ordered change, the more he makes it the same thing, so far as it can be made the same thing.

And this by the way: I often wonder what the Brighton man does when he wants a change. If he be the wealthier sort, the case is, of course, easy enough. He moves from a smart hotel on or near the Brighton front to a smart hotel in or near Piccadilly. And he again is perfectly at home; at Brighton-on-the-Park. But some of us, alas! are not smart, whatever our habitat, and I wonder whether the people who keep lodgings in the back blocks, the up-and-beyond of Brighton, know where to go when they are ordered a complete change. I can tell them. There is a region in London little known. It was once called Spa Fields; now it has no name, or none that I have ever heard. It is to be approached by going up the Gray's Inn Road some way north of Gray's Inn and then turning to the right. It has its Squares and its Crescents and its Places on the side of a steep hill; it has its

dusty little by-streets going off these more important avenues; it has its colonies of small shops,
its queer reminiscences and parodies on a small
scale of old-fashioned architectural modes; just
as in Brighton you come upon the most amusing
reproductions of the Pavilion in little. And here
is the odd thing. In the back parts of Brighton
and of other old-fashioned seaside places, it is
only by a strong exercise of the imagination that
you can believe that you are near the sea at all.
You can't see it — though your landlady may
have advertised that her apartments enjoy a fine
view of it. You can't see it, and nothing around
you looks like it. Everything is gritty, urban,
suburban, in its aspect. It is only faith, confidence in the scheme of the Universe, and an
assurance that the L.B. & S.C.R. would not
play a silly trick on you and go round and round
London and call Kentish Town Preston Park; it
is only a sure faith that prevents you saying:
'Why, this is Camden Town!' So, by an odd
reversal; it is only faith of the same sort, the
knowledge that life is real and life is earnest, as
Longfellow said, and not an Arabian Night, that
prevents you from looking out for a glimpse of
the sea from that London region of which I
have been speaking. You don't expect to see

much of it; you know that you are not in the
best quarters of the town, where the first floor
may run to anything; but you can't help feeling
that there must be a glimpse of the ocean visible
from the top windows of that house in Rouge-
mont Square. Actually, I am afraid, you would
only have a prospect of St. Pancras Railway
Station; still, the impression remains. And
hence I say: let the people at the back of Brighton who want a real change, take lodgings up in
this east-by-north of Gray's Inn quarter. They
will find it most refreshing; it is so much the
same thing.

And, lest I be accused of cheap superiority,
let me say that I believe most of these good
people, who change to remain the same, are
perfectly right. I don't think that the majority
of us are prepared for the real and tremendous
changes; I don't believe that such things would
do us any good. I feel no hankerings after St.
Helena; I do not wish to take a holiday on the
Plains of Alberta, Canada. It is true that most
of us are the better for a change; but it must
usually be a slight change to be beneficial, and,
often, a very slight change indeed. I have been
thinking of Guernsey this August, but I shall
not go there; for, if I did, I should stay there,

which would be out of the question. Guernsey would be a thorough change; and I am not thinking so much of the beautiful old town of St. Peter Port, where you mount a flight of stone steps to get from one street to another, nor of the lovely coast, nor of the sweet airs of the sea. For once I am a political man; I am thinking of the Guernsey Constitution. It seems perfect. The King was there last month, we know, and the royal visit led, naturally, to meditations on Guernsey on the part of the English papers. All of them spoke of the feudal ceremonies that were observed, of the seigneurs who put their hands between the hands of the Duke of Normandy — he also happens to be King of England — and swore to be his liegemen of life and limb, ready to defend him against all manner of folk. And then there was the matter of the lords who had to come through the water to greet their Duke, and of the lord who had to present two mallards, or wild ducks, with gilded bills, on a silver dish; and so with a number of beautiful old rites. But what I heeded was a short leading article in that fairest of papers, the *Manchester Guardian*. The *Guardian* was frankly puzzled with Guernsey. The *Guardian* represents the old school of Liberalism: the school of Bright and

Cobden — the school that at its worst was Grad-grind and Bounderby. And here, said the *Guardian*, was an island, boys and girls — just a little in the M'Choakumchild manner — which is happy, prosperous, loyal, contented. And yet the government of this island is in the hands of a High Bailiff, of the Jurats, elected for life, of the island parsons, and of a few officials. If the High Bailiff objects to a proposed measure, he vetoes it at once, and it is no more heard of. And, what the devil, boys and girls, the *Guardian* seemed to ask, if it could have used such language, does that island mean by being happy, loyal, prosper-ous, and contented under such an entirely pre-posterous Constitution? Now, as it happened, I was talking about the Guernsey Constitution and the *Manchester Guardian* article to a highly distinguished American. He is not obsolete, he was not born in a hot-bed of aristocratic pre-judices. I think I may say he is a live wire. And he said: 'I only wish we had the Guernsey Constitution in my country. We set out — and we meant well — to have a democracy. What we've got is a kakistocracy — a government by the worst men in the country.'

The American spoke on — he was eloquent like many of his countrymen — and showed, correctly, as I think, that politics and constitutions are a means, not an end, that the good and content and happiness of the people at large are the supreme end and law and reason of all governments; that the constitution of Guernsey was, therefore and evidently, perfect. Very likely he was right; and therefore I shall not take my holiday in Guernsey. I do not hold with violent changes, as I have said.

ROAST GOOSE

WITH A DISSERTATION ON APPLE SAUCE AND
SAGE AND ONIONS

*

THE war, I believe, is over. At all events, I will assume this to be the case, in order that I may speak of Michaelmas goose, and confess that, in common with most Englishmen, I have certain Teutonic tastes. In 1918, it was dangerous to admit a liking for Bach or Beethoven; now, I think, things are a little calmer, and I may venture to say that I like apple sauce with roast goose. As a matter of fact, I do not think that the goose, a very favourite dish in Germany, is served with apple sauce in that country; but the combination is purely Teutonic. In France, where dwells the True Church of cookery, they would shudder at the notion; just as they shudder at lamb and mint sauce and red-currant jelly with saddle of mutton and jugged hare. I know that these things are wrong; but I like them all the same; and they are all German in feeling. In Germany, as I have read, they serve raspberry jam with roast veal, and English travellers have been known to denounce the absurdity of the combination, not seeing that it is on all fours with their own saddle of mutton and currant jelly. I say again that these things are wickedness, but I like them very well, and all peoples who have any Teutonic blood in them love such mixtures. There is the 'Mostarda Soffrafina' of northern Italy; it is fruit — small pears, if I remember — pickled in a hot sweet sauce. This they eat in Lombardy with their boiled beef; and from this circumstance, if all the history books in the world had perished, we might infer that the Lombards were of Teutonic stock. So, I say, I am for apple sauce with the Michaelmas goose; and, let it be added, for the stuffing of sage and onions, which, so far as I know, is a purely English and a most happy thought. Here, again, we must differ from our masters in cookery, the French. Walking once in Touraine with a French friend, I saw a bush of sage growing by the roadside. I told the Frenchman the use to which it was put in England, in relation to the goose, the duck, and the pig. He nibbled a leaf, and then looked at me with a glance which I had met before in French company.

I had met it once from M. le Curê, on his learning from me that in England we pronounce 'Credo in unum Deum,' 'Creedo in yunum

Deeum,' instead of 'Craydo in oonoom Day-oom.' I met it again from a small farmer. We were talking in his vineyard, and as it happened, a great elderbush, laden with purple berries, grew at the corner of it. 'In England,' said I, ' we make those berries there into wine.' He glanced at me, and underlined his glance by spitting on the ground. And all three French-men intimated by this glance that they had always heard that the English were fools, and that now they were sure of it. Well, true friends can still be friends, in spite of differences; even if those differences are as vital and deep-reaching as the question raised by apple sauce and sage and onions with roast goose. And, since we are on the matter of stuffing, let us consider the traditional thyme and parsley stuffing which we in England dedicate to the fowl, the turkey, and to roast veal. We eat it because we like it, but science has discovered within the last few years that 'thymol' is a substance of high value. It is a powerful disinfectant, it is of great service to the digestive process, it is the very thing to give to the mucous membrane; and so we have been scientific without knowing it in eating thyme with our fowl. And so, no doubt, science will presently discover that Salvine – which is the

name that science will give to sage — is just as
good for us as thymol. And this opens a question which has always struck me as of curious
interest; the question of traditional wisdom in
meat, drink, and medicine. Long ago, before
chemistry in the modern sense can be said to
have existed, old women used to treat goitre by
rubbing a certain seaweed on the affected part.
The treatment was successful; and a few hundred
years afterwards science found that this seaweed
contained iodine, which is just the thing for
goitre. So with quinine. How did the savages
of South America find out that the bark of one
tree out of the thousands in their forests was
good for malaria? They did so; just as our fore-
fathers combined malt and hops into that admirable beverage, beer, without understanding in
the least that they were concocting a perfectly
balanced drink, which united the most valuable
nutritive and tonic constituents.

It is the process by which these results were
arrived at that puzzles me. Take the quinine,
for example. There is, I imagine, a vast choice
of trees and of plants in a South American forest.
Are we to imagine the Indian of past ages thread-
ing his way through this waste of wood, tasting
bits of trees, one after another, till he found the

cinchona and found that it eased his pains? And our old Englishwomen, with their seaweed for goitre: how on earth did they come to think of it? And the leaf that makes tea, and the berry that gives us coffee, and the plant that affords cocoa — the only end of which is chocolate — how are we to account for the discovery of their virtues? For with these, it is to be noted, the process is a complicated one. Not much satisfaction, one imagines, could be obtained by chewing the green leaves of the tea shrub; nor would the grinding of raw coffee berries between the teeth be of great service to body or mind. It must have been sheer intuition which told some wise man of thousands of years ago that the leaves of the tea plant must be dried, and that then boiling water must be poured upon them, and that the resultant liquor was good to drink. And so with tobacco; how did the poor Indian know that this was stuff to be smoked in a pipe? For all we can see, the Indians of Hindustan might well have smoked their tea leaves, and the Indians of America poured boiling water on their tobacco leaves. I remember, indeed, that Amundsen, the Arctic explorer, told me how he and his companions found that the tobacco had been forgotten at one of their 'dumps'; so they smoked tea in its place; but he did not speak well of the experiment. And I doubt whether tobacco tea would please a delicate palate. One must conceive primitive man, then, as engaged in endless dietetic and medicinal experiments; one must conceive him also as frequently feeling very unwell indeed; one must conceive him as occasionally dead. The man who wondered whether deadly nightshade would cure toothache, and made the experiment, fell a victim to the spirit of inquiry. And so, perhaps, there were anxious faces round the board when the first goose stuffed with sage and onions was eaten. It was a bold idea, all might be well; and, on the other hand, all might be very far from well.

All was well; and now, as I say, it only remains for science to prove that Salvine is the one preparation necessary to the happy digestion of the Michaelmas Goose.

WHERE ARE THE FOGS OF YESTERYEARS?

★

THIS is a degenerate age. All our comforts have either gone or are fast going. I have said so again and again. Nobody heeds me, or if I am heeded I am told to think of the telephone, the aeroplane, and tubular boilers. But what idle trifling is this? Whoever heard of a jolly party drinking punch as they sat about the sparkling, dancing telephone? Is there any true history of a party, weather-bound in an aeroplane, getting down at a cloud-tavern and telling stories to each other till they had compiled a *Household Words* or *All the Year Round* Christmas Number, only leaving the introduction, or framework, to be written by Mr. Dickens? Has a tubular boiler ever aided in the production of what John Browdie called something 'warm and varry coomfortable' to be taken after supper? Of course not; so what is the use of urging these idle conventions against my contention of the age's degeneracy?

All our comforts, I say, are passing from us. For here am I, writing in September and looking forward to October. Once on a time there would have been something to look forward to. For, with decent luck, and allowing for the eccentricities of our climate, the Londoner of twenty-five years ago had every reason to expect in October that rare treat, the first fog of the season. I must allow that the October fog was rarely, if ever, a perfect specimen of its kind. It was tender, it was, if you like, immature. It had not the richness of the right November growth. I do not think that I have ever heard of a man going past his own doorstep in a fog of October. The Great Fog Legend of the omnibus which somehow wandered into Clare Market — where is that market now? — was seen to vanish under an archway and was never seen more, belongs to November and Lord Mayor's Day. I admit, then, readily, that the amateur of fogs did not expect the great growths in October; but still there was a peculiar relish in the misty gifts of the month. A little thin, perhaps, in substance, a little lacking in the true sulphurous bouquet of later fogs; comparable, if you will, to the earliest duckling, to the August pear, but still, how relishable in their young and tender bloom! Wise men have held that a green goose eaten at Petertide has a delicacy of flavour that is wanting to the fatted bird of Michaelmas; and so there was a fleeting, sylph-like charm about the firstling fogs of October. The night before, perhaps, it had been warm and stuffy, and you began by casting off the second blanket on your bed. But somewhere in the small, mysterious hours, a chill came into the air and you half awoke, shivering slightly, and drew that rejected blanket back into its place and nestled gratefully under its genial warmth, and so fell asleep again and into happy dreams. And when the morning summons came, the light filtered dim and uncertain through the window, and, looking out, you saw not a street, but a white and fleecy cloud, through which rose the fantastic pinnacles of a fairy castle — otherwise, the chimney-pots of the houses over the way. And the noises of awakening London and the rattle of the rousing streets were hushed and muffled, as the whorls and eddies and wreaths of mist floated past your window. It had frozen in the night; and there was the exquisite result, the first fog of the year. And note the subtle relishes and aromas of this delicacy of the season. It was delightful in itself; for what can there be more delightful or of finer magic than an agency which turns Bloomsbury or Brixton into the appearance of a

cloud and the architecture thereof into a thing
of unearthly beauty? But beyond the actual
enjoyment that your first fog afforded, how rare
was it in its prophecy and promise of what was
to come! You looked forward to the great fogs
of November, December, January; to the masterpieces of foggery, when all London should pass
into the mighty cloud, when noon should be as
midnight, when the raw cold should pierce to
the very bone, when an errand to the shop round
the corner should be as desperate and doubtful
as an errand to the Pole, almost an occasion for
doorstep farewells; when huge blocks of ice
should grind together in the invisible Thames,
when the curtain of thick Egyptian darkness, if
it were lifted for a moment, should show vast
caverns and antres of tawny, fiery light, as it
were the glow of a dying furnace. Such were the
happy anticipations of that October morning of
the past.

But, as I said once or twice before, our comforts and our simple pleasures are taken from
us one by one. There are no real fogs in London
now; the dimness of October gives no promise
of November darkness. The last real fog was
'presented' on or about December 23, 1904. It
was not a fog of the first class, for it was pure

white and rigorists might maintain that it was merely a thick river mist. But the hansom cabmen were leading their horses, lamps went before the crawling omnibuses, and some guests, bidden to a wedding feast, went past one of the biggest London hotels without seeing it. Call it a mist if you will; but when shall we have such a mist again? And, just as I was going to write — for the third or fourth time — that life and London have few comforts left in them, it suddenly strikes me that there may be people who will declare that the London fogs of olden time were not comforts at all, but gross discomforts and miseries; that, in short, we are all the better and more comfortable without them. Well, I love a good paradox, but this is a little too much, even for me. The proposition that would deny the curious pleasures of a London fog is not a paradox; it is not even an oxymoron; it is a piece of rank absurdity. Surely this is obvious. I remember once talking to a great Arctic explorer. It was a day of piercing cold — what we in London call piercing cold — and there was a glorious and tremendous fire on the hearth. Before this fire the great man stood displayed, as I think the heralds say, in his enjoyment of the light, of the glow, of the crackling coals, and the genial heat. His face beamed like the blaze behind it, brightened like the light of the flames that danced on the dull walls. 'You know,' said he, 'that nobody who has not been up to his waist in the freezing slush of the Arctic can enjoy a fire like this.' Of course not; I saw his point at once. The argument surely needs not to be laboured; it is clear enough that the comforts of life cannot be enjoyed without the apposition of their contraries. You do not hear of the people of Aden or Bagdad or Bassorah — I prefer the old spelling — gathering about a glowing, roaring fire, drinking hot punch, and thanking Heaven for these delights. And since man is evidently meant to sit at flaming hearths and to drink hot punch, it is clear that if circumstances forbid his enjoyment of these pursuits he is so far a maimed and imperfect creature, deprived of the comforts in which he was intended to take his pleasure. Should we not then all become Arctic explorers?

That, no doubt, were the right and manly course; but there are difficulties in the way, and one can conceive objections being raised to the population of London spending the season round the North and South Poles. It would interfere with the films and with many social fixtures. In the old days there was a happy middle course. We had the fogs of which I have been speaking; with what a relish we drew back the curtains and saw the air grow dark without as the fire blazed bright within. The bitterer the chill of the air, the more grateful the warmth; the deeper the gloom without, the happier the hearts within. Decidedly, a London fog was one of the choicest of comforts.

But now, as Mr. Micawber said, when he was released from prison, everything is gone from us.

In the infancy of photography, the artist with the camera was accustomed to say to his patients: 'Smile, please.' In those days one had to assume rigidity for a considerable time before the releasing 'Thank you' was uttered; and so it was no wonder that these frozen and prolonged smiles came out in a somewhat ghastly manner, and render many an old family album a terror and a wonder to this day. But this is beside the point. I merely recall the photographer of 1869–70, because I am reversing his favourite injunction. I do not say 'Smile, please.' I say: 'Be so kind as to look grave.' For we are to have a little theology.

It comes about like this. Somebody – I forget his name and the name of his book – has just written an amusing work about the eminent men of our age. He 'takes them off,' I gather, with a pretty wit, and dealing with Mr. G. K. Chesterton, gives a pleasant version of the Chestertonian doctrine; that no one without a bottle of Bass in each hand can enter the Kingdom of Heaven. And the curious thing is that he is evidently under the impression that he has uttered an extravagant paroody of G. K. C., that he has reduced his position to an absurdity. Well, I cannot answer for Mr. Chesterton, but if I were he, I should accept the intended sarcasm as an admirable statement of my case; condensed, no doubt, and familiar, in its illustration, but all the better for that. Of course a man cannot enter the Kingdom of Heaven without a bottle of Bass in each hand. Advanced theologians, Modernists, Universalists and all that lot may hold that one bottle in one hand may just scrape a man past the gates, but I have never had much sympathy with what is called Liberal theology. But, surely, the supposed absurd and damaging overstatement is merely the most obvious and the soundest common sense. For, sinking the technical expression of the doctrine – I am afraid pure theology is apt now and then to degenerate into asperity, and I must not get cross in these calm pages – what reason is there to suppose that a good man is one who is devoid of a palate and devoid of a stomach; devoid, in fact, of senses of any kind? It having pleased Heaven to give its creatures these faculties of sense, why should we think that Heaven will be highly gratified by our behaving as if we had no such faculties? A man who blandly but firmly declined to admit that the sun was bright or the sky was blue, on the ground that good men never saw anything, would run the risk of being certified. Why whould a man who pretends that he can't taste anything be thought to be a being of a superior caste? For, be it noted, I am not pressing the pro-alcohol side of the argument. 'Bass,' as I take it, means something good to drink, without reference to the fact that if you drink too much of that agreeable beverage you may be led to commit indiscretions. For the moment, I am willing to substitute for 'a bottle of Bass in each hand,' 'an exquisitely made cup of chocolate in each hand,' and that beverage reminds me of the story told by the great French gourmet, Brillat Savarin. That most sensible man, reviewing the Revolution from his special point of view, deplored the ruin that it brought to the monasteries and the convents. These, he said, speaking from experience, were the great schools of the last refinements in cookery, and he quotes the dictum of an Abbess of his acquaintance on this very subject of chocolate. 'If you would have chocolate in perfection, my dear sir,' said the religious lady, 'if you would taste its most exquisite aromas, you must make it overnight and warm it up again the next morning; and I am sure that the good God, in whom reside all perfections, will not grudge us this little refinement.' The Abbess was in the right of it. It is, of course, true that a really good man does not suffer his liking for a bottle of Bass or a cup of chocolate to make him neglect his mother, starve his wife, or send his children to the workhouse. If a good man has to choose between making the chocolate overnight and suffering the wife of his bosom to experience the pangs of want, he will, almost always, say: 'By all means make it in the morning; I can bear it.' But this is true of all delights of the senses; a really nice man will not suffer his family to come to grief in order that he may indulge his propensity for looking at sunsets.

I said that we would waive the more or less alcoholic side of the question as involved in the symbol, 'Bass,' selected by Mr. Chesterton's critic. I said so because I think that good drink merely represents the first line of the cause which the bad people are attacking. It is my opinion that these bad people are only in the first stage or movement of a much more general attack. Tobacco will be the next line, the next engagement will centre round the meditative pipe, the gay cigarette, the magnificent Corona.

Already that battle is preparing in America;
soon, in powerful circles, a pipe will be inconsis-
tent with piety. Nor will matters stop there.
The Vegetarians have long been aware that
what is the matter with the world is Meat.
They have their feelings, like the anti-Burgundy
and anti-Bass people and the anti-Tobacco
people. They are quite convinced, with Mr.
Bumble in *Oliver Twist*, that Meat is the root
of all evil.

'It's not Madness, ma'am,' replied Mr.
Bumble . . . 'it's Meat.'

These persons then, sharing the opinion and
the intelligence of Mr. Bumble, will engage on
an anti-meat campaign. If they win, they will
divide into two parties. One set will allow us to
cook our vegetables; the other side will insist that
if you are to boil your green peas, you may as
well dine off rumpsteak at once. And, of course,
sham science will come to their aid. There are
plenty of doctors already who are quite prepared
to demonstrate by unanswerable arguments that
if you cook anything you destroy all its value.
Before long there will be letters in *The Times* over
signatures furnished with the most appalling
array of degrees and qualifications showing that
the way out of all our difficulties is to put out the

94

kitchen fire.[1] But it would be a great mistake to suppose that the campaign will stop here, with our palates and stomachs and general comfort and well-being. All the arts will next be the object of attack; tobacco, beer, beef and boiled beans having fallen, painting, sculpture, music, literature will be suspected, examined, denounced, prohibited. This is no fantasy; for this has happened before. It happened in the sixteenth and seventeenth centuries, and is generally known as Puritanism. The movement was then allied with certain theological views. It began by smashing and destroying all the beautiful things that were then to be found in churches. It blotted out of the world a mass of beauty in a manner which is really awful to

[1] I was a true prophet. The above was written in 1921. Now, in 1923, I have just been reading the report of a lecture by Dr. Leonard Williams, a well-known Harley Street specialist. Dr. Williams declares that the kitchen range is the worst enemy of man, and that we ought to live on raw roots and things, and very little of them. Compare with this the system of another distinguished specialist, Mr. Squeers, of Dotheboys Hall, Yorkshire. 'When a boy gets weak and ill and don't relish his meals we give him a change of diet — turn him out for an hour or so every day into a neighbour's turnip-field, or sometimes, if it's a delicate case, a turnip-field and a piece of carrots alternately.'

contemplate. Macaulay, not by any means the acutest of critics in a general way, got to the heart of the matter in his account of the Puritan objection to bear-baiting. They disliked bear-baiting, he said, not because it gave pain to the bear, but because it gave pleasure to the specta-tors. So with their objection to sports and games of all sorts. They began by saying – and, no doubt, believing – that games were wicked when played on Sunday. They ended by banning games and sports of all kinds on any day. They shut up the theatres: they gave pleasure, and the Puritan hates pleasure because it is a good thing.

Now at the end of this grave sermon, I will give my text, reserving it, contrary to the usual practice of sound divines, to the last. This is the month of November, and on the eleventh of November is the feast of St. Martin, that good soldier-saint who gave half his cloak to the shivering beggar. And in the old days they used to say:

On the feast of Martinmas
Cups of ale shall freely pass.

They knew in those days that the saint and his charity and good ale were all good together, each in its several degree. They knew that

96

all three were 'congruous.' They knew that
a man cannot enter the Kingdom of Heaven
unless he carries a bottle of Bass in each
hand.

CHRISTMAS MUMMING

★

I HAVE often been tempted to put a certain question to the Vicar: to any vicar. Does he in his heart think that anything has much changed in the last four or five thousand years — that is in the known course of history? Are we any better; are we any worse? On the whole, if the said vicar had a parish in Babylon, would the general conduct of his parishioners have been much different from that of his parishioners in his parish in Marylebone? Or supposing him to be a country vicar; wouldn't he be glad on the whole if his young people were as decent in their ways as Daphnis and Chloe?

It is a large question, and I have had grave doubts on the matter; but, lately looking up this business of Christmas, I am inclined to think that we really have got on a little. But, first, it is necessary to go into the origin of Christmas. The old story was that it was a peculiarly northern festival; that all its mirth and jollity and ringing carols and sumptuous meats and drinks had no reference to any Christian joy. All our Christmas mirth, these wise men told us, we had inherited from our Scandinavian ancestors, who had noted that the tide of winter began to turn for the better somewhere about our Christmastide. The shortest day was past, the hours of light steadily began to lengthen, the spring was already prophesied. And so the Northern people literally made a song and dance about it; they made merry because the worst of the winter was over, and better things were coming. It is all very ingenious; but I think I see flaws. Did these people who rejoiced at Christmas tear their hair on Midsummer Day because the longest day was over and winter would soon be upon them? I have never heard that they did anything of the kind. And, again, it may be objected that the worst of the winter is, demonstrably, not over at Christmas. In nine cases out of ten the worst is to come. They must have been simple souls, indeed, those Scandinavians, if they rejoiced for winter past in December; with the terrors of January, February, and, often, of March to come. As a matter of fact, of course, they made merry as we make merry at this season, so far as our mirth is seasonal at all, precisely for the opposite reason. 'It is very cold, indeed: the snow is falling fast, the

99

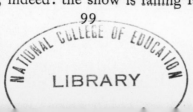

wind comes piercing from the North, all appearances of summer are long over: and the best of it is, there is greater cold to come.' That is the real sentiment of the season, and De Quincey expresses it admirably. Thus he writes, indicating the season and the circumstances of felicity:

'Let it, however, not be spring, nor summer, nor autumn — but winter in his sternest shape. This is a most important point in the science of happiness. And I am surprised to see people overlook it, and think it matter of congratulation that winter is going, or if coming, is not likely to be a severe one. . . . Indeed, so much of an epicure am I in this matter, that I cannot relish a winter night fully if it be much past St. Thomas's day, and have degenerated into disgusting tendencies to vernal appearances; no, it must be divided by a thick wall of dark nights from all return of light and sunshine.'

And that, no doubt, is the truth of the matter, expressed as only that wonderful, profound and eloquent De Quincey could express it. But there is another point to be noted: they kept up Christmas tremendously in pagan Rome, though they did not call it by that name. Now, winter has no frightful terrors in Italy, and yet, it is odd enough, the Christmas of Rome fell, within a day or two, just at our Christmas-tide. They called it the Saturnalia. The *Classical Dictionary* tells me that it was a feast of immemorial antiquity, founded to commemorate the golden, happy age of Saturn. 'All animosity ceased, schools were shut, war was never declared, but all was mirth, riot and debauchery.' The last phrase is a little severe, but I think we may take it as meaning that the ancient Romans had a thoroughly good time at this season of the year. All social inequalities were annulled while the feast lasted; and as in old Virginia, in the slavery days, the black people claimed the right of taking the inside places in the coaches at Christmas while their masters rode outside, so in Rome, the slave told his master what he thought of him. 'Come,' says Horace to his man, 'use your December liberty, say what you like.' The man used it, freely enough; he told his master what he thought of him; that nobody would have been unhappier than he if he had suddenly found himself in the good old times that he was always praising, and so forth. Davus, in fact, told his master home truths, and it is in this point that, I claim, we have advanced over ancient morals. For, be it observed, we use our December liberty in quite another sense. Christmastide is exactly the season when we keep what are called home truths in the background. We hold back all the nasty things that are at the tip of our tongues, we begin to find that there is a good deal to be said for 'that scoundrel Brown,' we discover that M'Caw's cold and studied insolence is 'only manner,' and that Mulligan's noisy and tiresome vulgarity is pure heartiness and high spirits. We find out, in short, that we are all jolly good fellows. Even a man who considers himself deeply injured thinks it all over at Christmas, and sees that there is something to be said on the other side. And thus we transcend and surpass the pagan conception of Christmas – or Saturnalian – jollity. The Romans told each other 'home truths'; we tell each other *the* truth. For, of course, we *are*, all of us, jolly good fellows. Consider, if we speak of literature; what is the truth about it? Surely, that is to be sought in Shakespeare, and Keats, not in the commercial drama of the West End, nor in the feeble imbecilities of the minor poets. If we are to speak of painting, we mean Turner, we neglect the existence of German oleographs and all the multitude of pink sentimentalities in pigment. Architecture means Westminster Abbey, not a tin meeting house. It is the good things and the splendid things and the perfect things that come to the account; not the failures or make-believes. So, with ourselves and the rest of us: at Christmas we see humanity as it ought to be: genial, full of charity, brimming over with mirth and good will. We are mummers, if you please; we dress up, if you like: but we know that these gay, cheerful and resplendent vestments are the clothes that we should always wear, if things were right, if 'the letters of the Name were made known.' It is true that one cannot go by the Underground into the City in parti-coloured jester's robes, or in the silver armour of St. George: but so much the worse for the Underground and the City.

At Queen's College, Oxford, they bring in the Boar's Head with surpliced songmen and choristers and a noble old carol at Christmas. Everybody knows in his heart that this is the way in which we should always dine, if the world were properly managed. In the rush of business, it would be slightly inconvenient if the chops and steaks and cuts from the joint were brought in by chanting waiters: still, the old Oxford Christmas custom shows how the thing should be done.

> The boar's head in hand bear I
>   Bedecked with bays and rosemary.
> And I pray you, my masters, be merry
>   *Qui estis in convivio*
> *Caput apri defero*
>   *Reddens laudes Domino.*

A TALK FOR TWELFTH NIGHT

★

WE have been talking a lot of one Will Shakespeare lately. Miss Clemence Dane wrote not long ago a play about him. Mr. Arthur Whitby,[1] one of the actors in it, an old Bensonian of ripe and large experience, and as well-graced a player as any we have in these days, told me that never had he been called upon to deliver such beautiful lines upon the stage — save when he had to speak the verse written by Shakespeare himself. And all kinds of fine things have been spoken of the piece, and yet it did not run — principally, I think, because the critics took it into their heads on the first night that Shakespeare was represented as Marlowe's murderer. Now, I never saw 'Will Shakespeare,' so I must say nothing of its presentation, or of the stage management which allowed this tavern scuffle between the two dramatists to be dubious and obscure: but I am a little entertained at the — implied — horror in the criticisms. Supposing Miss Clemence Dane had really made Shakespeare get into a rage with his rival, Marlowe, and draw that

[1] Since dead, alas!

little dagger which hung by every man's side in those days and stab Marlowe to the heart: what about it? Should we have any reason to be shocked or surprised or alarmed or disgusted if such had been the fact, not merely in the twentieth-century play, but in sixteenth-century real life? Didn't Ben Jonson kill his man? Does anybody suppose that Shakespeare, the social being of his age, was any better than Ben Jonson, any better than the average Elizabethan playwright? Really it is time that we cleared our minds of this cant about Shakespeare; it is worse than the Scottish cant about Burns, a noble poet and a capital fellow in many ways, but — in actual life — not always in the Cotter's Saturday Night frame of mind.

Now, be patient. Examine yourself, and, speaking by custom of confession, avow that you hold Shakespeare to have been all good and all knowing and all wise; the genius being taken for granted. In spite of Ben Jonson's fervent but most truthful eulogy you insist that he had all the science of the age at his command. It has been quite in vain that the good Ben insisted that Will's education was a mere smattering — 'small Latin and less Greek'

— you will have it that the creator of Falstaff must have been to some Dotheboys Hall of the period, where he was 'instructed in all languages living and dead, mathematics, orthography, geometry, the use of the globes, algebra, single-stick (if required), writing, arithmetic, fortification, and every other branch of classical literature.' Now, this was not the case. I have just been turning up his January play, 'Twelfth Night.' I look over the cast. The scene is laid in Illyria, which is now Jugo-Slovakia. Most of the names are Italian, which passes very well: but what about 'Sir Toby Belch, uncle to Olivia,' and his friend, 'Sir Andrew Aguecheek'? Are Belch and Ague-cheek names often found on the Illyrian sea-board? Most certainly not in the year 1600; possibly now, if the Gloucestershire Belches and the Westmorland Aguecheeks have small fixed incomes and are able to take advantage of the extremely favourable rate of exchange in Jugo-Slovakia. This is a small instance. But it does illustrate, and prove, the position that the true Shakespeare was not the creature of the intellectual and moral tea-party that we imagine. He laughs at all the schoolmasters. I dare say he knew that people on the Illyrian seaboard had, as a rule, Italian sounding names. What did he care? When he wanted broad comic effects from his characters he gave them gross and ridiculous English names — because he knew that these names would incline the pit to mirth. The 'high brow,' the 'intellectual,' the 'intelligentsia' would rather perish than use such a device: but Shakespeare — or 'Shagsper,' if you like — was not of that world. I have often thought that one of the finest pieces of Shakespearean criticism that I have ever heard came from my old friend, Jerome K. Jerome. I was talking to him about the libraries, especially the German libraries, that had been written on Shakespearean psychology.

'Shakespeare,' said Jerome, 'was not like that. When he had got all those people dead in the last scene in "Hamlet," he struck a flourish with his pen, and said to himself: "There! that ought to bring 'em in!"'

And there no doubt you have a great deal of the root of the matter. Shakespeare was not, consciously, a moralist, a philosopher, a thinker. He was a Warwickshire lad, with a small scholastic grounding and a universal curiosity, who came up to town and, somehow, fell into the theatre business first as actor, then as playhouse author, then as speculator — he was a member of the little syndicate that took up the land in Southwark on which the Globe was built. In addition, he happened to be a man of the supremest genius. But the chief passion of his life was Stratford-on-Avon. He never forgot it. Amid all the wild whirl of that London life — and it was a wild whirl then, a foaming torrent of such passions, political, sensual, emotional, intellectual, that our poor attempts at being alive in London now are pretty much as the green stuff on a duck-pond is to Niagara — he thought of the friendly fires and the good taverns and the solid, stolid, worthy people and the beloved fields. 'Romeo and Juliet,' 'Hamlet,' 'Othello,' — so many steps nearer to the haven where he would be, to the true, secure life that he loved. We think our London a tremendous centre of excitement; we, who are impressed when somebody takes hold of a revue which is a failure and turns it into a revue which is a success! Rubbish! William Shakespeare lived in a London which was impressed when it saw live men disembowelled at Tyburn, and heads of traitor nobles spiked on London Bridge. He lived in a red-hot world; a world of terrific beauty, horror, cruelty, disgust, revelry; our tea-party people and commentating Dons do not begin to have the elementary data — as they would say — for the understanding of Shakespeare. I do not believe that many of them have read Ben Jonson's description of a voyage down Fleet Ditch; they had better not; it would make them unwell. But it is, no doubt, this imbecile notion of what Shakespeare ought to have been — a Don who condescended to write plays — that has led to the more imbecile notion that he could not have been the son of a Stratford shopkeeper who prospered none too well, and did not keep the roadway in front of his shop any too clean. To the horrible people who are best distinguished as Dons, whose idea of heaven is an everlasting examination, it is repulsive that this young wastrel, with a possible Grammar School smattering, should have written the finest things in the world. 'The Warwickshire yokel,' says one of them, in high contempt. Clearly impossible that such a person should have written plays which we annotate with innumerable 'cf.'s' and infinitely tiresome and irrelevant information, plays which we conduct examinations on, concerning which we write infinite dissertations. This author could have been no Stratford vagabond, no miserable player; he must have been one of us. And so has arisen the most marvellous folly of the world; the Baconian hypothesis. Grave men, being first assured that shabby, 'Bohemian' fellows do not write immortalities, have committed themselves to all the wonderful lunacies of the bi-literal cypher, have gone a little farther, and have at last found that Bacon wrote, not only all Shakespeare, but all the literature of the age, not only English, but foreign, including Montaigne's *Essays*, and Cervantes' *Don Quixote*. The last book which I read on the subject showed that *Don Quixote* should be read 'd'un qui s'ôte' — concerning one who hides himself — Bacon, of course. Indeed, the writer proved that the alleged author, Cervantes, had an illegitimate child and was very poor.

Which is evidence, of course, that he could not write masterpieces. The masterpieces notoriously are all written by moral men with large banking accounts.

May this January, this Twelfth Night, bring us better sense, as we sit about our sea-coal fire.

★

THE other day a sad case came before the courts; one of those cases in which 'the home' has been broken up owing to differences, disagreements, subjects of variance and quarrel. Such affairs are not uncommon, though they are not quite so common as the members of the Society for the Instant Abolition of the Family pretend; but in the case of which I am speaking there were highly uncommon elements. Husband and wife had parted, not on account of the fabled lodger, or for any such simple cause. It was astrology that had driven them apart; it was astrology that sent the wife to dwell in the workhouse. I think that it was the lady who began it. I believe that she and her mother had dealt deeply in the Twelve Houses of the Heavens, in Rising Signs, in Lords of the Ascendant, in Trine and Sextile. At any rate, during the war, a communication came from astrological or other occult regions to the effect that the wife would be killed by an explosion. The husband, who had evidently become a fervent believer, met this threat with a scheme of his own. He caused his wife to sleep in the kitchen, and, as it were, bid the stars come on. Here, you may say, is one of the oddest instances of the mad irrationalities which infest the human mind. The husband believed in the stars and their doom, and he thought that this august fate, written in the heavens, this sentence issuing, we will suppose, from Mars ill-aspected with the Sun, could be turned aside and annulled — by a thin basement ceiling! Absurd enough, certainly; and yet no more absurd than the conduct of the father and mother of Œdipus in the Greek play. They were informed by the oracle that the child born to them would murder his father and marry his mother; and so — believing in the Oracle with all their hearts — they exposed the infant on a desolate mountain. It didn't do; you could not get round Greek Oracles that way, though you may play fast and loose with English horoscopes.

But to return to our modern family. The evidence as reported seems to become vague; all that was clear was that husband and wife, through roaming too freely in the starry plains, drifted apart on the earthly ones; and so the process of the courts drops a dull curtain on a curious scene. But the interest of all this to me was the survival of the belief in astrology; in that system which declares, sometimes in extreme terms, sometimes in moderate phrases, that human life is ruled by the planets; that things in Park Lane and Peckham, Brixton and Belgravia, Aldgate and Mayfair, all depend upon the march of Sun and Moon, Mars, Mercury, Venus, and the rest of them. It is an astounding theory. Here, we will say, is a little boy with a racking cough and an anxious mother bending over him; Saturn is 'afflicting the Native.' At the same time, Smith takes to his breast Beauty and Half-a-Million; Mercury and the Moon have fulfilled their promise to him. And Uranus, aided by Mercury, now in a very different humour, shuts up the small grocer's shop in Norwood and sends the grocer — poor man — off to the Bankruptcy Court.

There, in the rough, is the system. The broad lines of your life are all settled at the moment of your birth; success or failure, happiness or misery, riches or poverty, early death or length of days; all these are patent to the astrologer's eye. Give him but the moment of birth; his predictions will extend to the day of death. And the odd thing is: that while the astrologer's art has been known to the world certainly six thousand years, probably for a much longer time – they had horoscopes and bearer-cheques and bills-of-sale, all in bricks, in Babylon – yet mankind has never yet been able to make up its mind definitely whether there is anything in it, or whether it is all stuff and nonsense.

Not really to make up its mind. Certainly, the eighteenth century pooh-poohed the whole business, just as it pooh-poohed Alchemy. But that was more an impatient gesture than a reasoned conviction. The eighteenth century pooh-poohed Gothic Architecture in a similar manner. Gothic has long come to its own again; and they tell me that there are great commercial possibilities before Alchemy – or 'Synthetic Gold' – in Germany. At any rate, the principle of alchemy, the artificial transmutation of metals, has long been recognized by modern science. And, then, coming to my own experience: I once knew an astrologer. He predicted nothing so far as I was concerned. But one day, in the midst of casual conversation, he remarked, quietly enough:

'You have received two interesting letters in the course of the week, since I last saw you. One dealt with the discomforts of theatrical travelling. The other was about a particular article in the *Classical Dictionary*. And last Sunday you were talking to some people about the fooleries of your occult friends.'

There it was. It was all true. How did he do it? I don't know. He said it was astrological A B C. It struck me that a very rough-and-ready test might be to my hand in the February Calendar, in the list of the great born during that month. For, if the general principles of astrology were true, it would probably follow that each month would have its own type. There would be the Februarian man, the Martian man, the Augustan man, and so forth. I did not, somehow, expect to find much confirmation in the February Calendar. But I found it.

The three most eminent names of those born in February are Charles Dickens, Henry Irving, and Ellen Terry. The most distinguished actor and actress of the last age; and the great Dickens, whose passion for the stage was almost a disease! I am sure that it was only the immense common sense of Dickens, the servant of his genius – as it often is – that prevented him from joining Crummles early in life. And he was an enthusiastic amateur

all his days; his theatrical exploits make but
tiresome reading. But there you are: it really
looks as if the February aspects of the heavens
inclined strongly to the theatre. Yet, for my
part, I do not believe a word of it. Astrology
cannot be true: for, if it were true, life would
be impossible. Human nature, as we know it,
would perish away and blacken as a piece of
tissue paper in a candle flame. We could not
live, if we knew what our life was to be. We
could form no plans if their futility were plain
from the start. And how about racing? I know
racing men pretend that they deal in 'certs,'
even in 'dead certs.' I have listened to them
conferring together and proving beyond a
shadow of doubt that the arrival of Bolter at
the winning-post in advance of all others is as
sure a thing as the arrival of the sun over the
horizon in the morning. Well, the race is run
and Bolter is nowhere in particular; but in a
week's time the same group will be talking in
the same terms of Wolter or Polter or Nolter.
They only deal in ' certs.'

But, of course, in their hearts they must be
quite well aware that their 'certs' are really
'uncerts.' If it were otherwise betting would be
dead in a day. You can't wager your money on

the number of days in the week or the number of weeks in the year or on the multiplication table. There must be some sort of a chance, or there can be no bet. But if astrology were true, it would be A B C, I suppose, for the skilled astrologer to forecast every race by the immutable laws of the heavens. Whereupon, the Turf and all that it implies would instantly cease to exist. And I submit that, as Britons, we know that this would be absurd.

Therefore, Astrology is all stuff and nonsense!

*

I WAS going to write some fierce and eloquent things about March weather: about the days that grow longer and yet drearier, about the leaden heavens, the villainous wind from the north-east which comes from far, unhappy Siberian plains and searches to the very marrow of the bones, and about the March dust which swirls about the pavements, afflicting the eyes, choking mouth and nostrils. Our light-hearted ancestors used to say that a peck of this March dust was worth a king's ransom; but they lived on the land and measured life, largely, by the land. They knew nothing of what that dust can do in Piccadilly and the Strand. In fine, I was going to be savage with March and with Charles Kingsley, who was perverse enough to write a poem in praise of that horrible north-east wind, which sent him at last to his grave. And then, calling up memories of bygone March weather, I changed my mind. The sort of article which I had in mind would look silly, read in a deck-chair placed securely in garden shade, while the young people played lawn tennis in the full blaze and glow of the sun, and

119

mopped their brows, calling for more ice in the cup. Yet that might well happen. Exactly forty years ago, I remember that there was just such weather in March; almost a week of it. A cloudless blue sky morning after morning, a delicious warmth in the sunlight, and that brilliance in the air which we do not often see in London — or in England either for the matter of that — that brilliance which reminds me always of Touraine and Provence, in which everything seen is clearly and sharply defined, in which every object seems to sparkle, as if it were not only in the light but was itself a form of light: all these signs were to be seen in those days of March, 1882. All the shops put out their awnings, people sauntered happily in this happy summer air, and lawn tennis — a youngish game then — flourished in that wonderful March weather. We all took the snowstorm which ended the spell as an outrage.

So again in '93, the year of the King's marriage — there were real music-halls in London in those days, and Charles Godfrey was singing two songs, 'After the Ball' and a loyal chant about 'Georgy-Porgy, Duke of Yorky' — in the year 1893 summer began in March and continued without a break till autumn. Then,

again, only two years ago March in London
was like July in Penzance; warm, still air and
a constant dropping of fine warm rain; the
sort of weather which gardeners like for bud-
ding-roses and taking cuttings. My pear tree –
the pear tree – was a white cloud of shining
glory that year on St. Patrick's Day; and my
fern – *the* fern – had sent up its young growth
with the fronds curved like a bishop's crozier
five or six inches above ground. So, on the
whole, it is best to leave March well alone; to
say nothing about that vile north-easter, those
bitter and grievous skies, the abominable
scourge of the blinding, stinging dust. March
may be anything or everything: it is only
constant in its inconstancy – like the remaining eleven months of our blessed English
year.

And hence the interest which we take in our
weather. Foolish and proud people often re-
proach us with talking overmuch about the
weather. 'A fine day, isn't it, for March?'
'Gorgeous June weather!' 'A very seasonable
Christmas': these remarks, and many others
like them, are supposed to indicate the depths
of banality and stupidity on the part of the
speakers. 'They can talk about nothing except

the weather,' say the proud and foolish ones. These would like us to talk about Mrs. Humphry Ward, *The Story of an African Farm*, Nietzsche, Bergson, Psycho-Analysis, Relativity. They do not realize that it is they themselves who are the frivolous chatterers, occupied with the passing, the transient, the radically unimportant. What price – if I may be familiar for a moment – *Robert Elsmere* to-day? How many people in a hundred can tell me what happened at that African Farm? And as to the *élan vital*, now? And where do you think Psycho-Analysis will be in 1932? With crinolines and gigot sleeves – and *Robert Elsmere*. But we shall still be talking about the weather. And rightly: for our English weather is a matter of perennial interest. This, be it noted, is by no means the case with all weather. Don't tell a Southern Spaniard in August what a sunny day it is; he would invoke his saints against you. It is unwise to greet an Anglo-Indian on the plains at breakfast with, 'Another splendid day!' for if you do his liver will burn with angry bile, as Horace says of another matter, and he will hate you. I do not know what an Eskimo would say if you remarked to him: 'Snowy, isn't it?' in December. But he would not be interested. Note the distinction. In the Arctic region and on the Indian plain, weather talk is banal, empty and ridiculous. Here the sun never fails to blaze and scorch, there the snow surely falls. There is nothing to be said. To comment on the weather in such lands is as if one remarked: 'The sun rose this morning,' or 'The angles at the base of an isosceles triangle are equal.' But in England the case is altogether different. The Englishman may justly note that it is a fine day for March and that it is gorgeous June weather and so forth — just because there is no possibility of his encountering the answer: 'Of course it is.' It is never, of course. It froze in the southern counties in August a year and a half ago; and I must confess that the blaze of sunlight and the figures of the thermometer last October frightened me. There was something almost Apocalyptic about such weather. I remember especially noting the incongruity between the position of the sun in the sky with its heat and brilliance. Morning and evening it was low in the heavens, for such is the place of the sun in October; and yet its heat was vehement and its light blazed in the eyes as if we had been in the high dog-days. And on the other hand, there is the old tale of the Derby, run, not in a snowstorm, but — as I am assured — between two flurries of snow. Hence the perpetual interest of the English weather. It abounds in differences, in the unexpected; and it is only such things which are truly interesting, significant and beautiful. All the relish of life, or almost all of it, is to be sought in the element of surprise.

And this, let it be observed, is one of the few universal axioms that apply to everything; to nature, to man, to art. Let us consider, for example, the case of Jones, of London Wall and Surbiton, and the case of the starry heavens. Take Jones. We avoid him when we can. We let him choose his own carriage in the 9.30; and then get into another. The reason is that Jones never fails to say the expected thing. His conversation can be foretold with a degree of accuracy that the Meteorological Department of the Air Service has never attained in dealing with the weather. You always know exactly what he will say on any possible subject. A good man is Jones in every relation of life, and his pink peonies are the pride of Surbiton, Hampton, Molesey and the Dittons; but avoid him, since he lacks the element of surprise;

in Bacon's words, there is no 'strangeness in the proportion' of Jones. He lacks that quality which the man who didn't write Shakespeare's works saw was essential to true beauty – or, we may add, to true significance and interest. And then, with this rule and measure of things still in our hands, let us contemplate the midnight sky of a clear, frosty night. An awful spectacle indeed, as Carlyle is supposed to have observed; but a spectacle awful in its wonder and its beauty – in its infinite diversity of form. Consider how the heavens would appear if the stars had been arranged in a definite and formal pattern of geometrical design, with everything matching and corresponding. *That* would be an awful spectacle in another sense; a spectacle as awful as a model prison or the corridors of a modern hotel. We could not have borne to look upon it. Indeed, there are modern streets that we can hardly bear to look upon, long, straight streets that go off from main roads in the far east of London, almost vanishing in perspective. They are terrible, these streets, because they consist of one house repeated, as it seems, to infinity. From end to end there is no variety, no element of surprise, in these dreary ways; hence, if we can, we

avoid them as we avoid Jones of London Wall
and Surbiton.

Hence, on the other hand, the charm and
delight of things made by hand as contrasted
with things made mechanically. Mark the
difference between a bit of ironwork that has
been hammered out by a craftsman, and another
bit of ironwork that has been cast from the same
design. In the latter case, absolute uniformity
of execution, twirl and twist and curve corresponding with twirl and twist and curve to
the tenth of an inch. In the former, infinite
difference, endless though slight variety; no
two twirls or twists exactly or absolutely alike.
And you will find, if you care to examine the
matter closely, that an oak tree is constructed
on the same principle as the craftsman's ironwork. No two leaves on that tree are exactly
alike, though there is a close general resem-
blance between all the leaves on the broad tree.
And here I am reminded that with all the good-
will in the world, one must not write about
our English weather and omit to have a dig
at it. So, be it observed, the difference between
the leaves on the oak tree and the curly-
wurlies on the iron gates are slight differences.
The pattern in the ironwork 'matches,' though

not absolutely; the leaves of the oak are very like one another, though not the same. I should not like to see fronds of a tree-fern sprouting from the boughs of our stout native oak.

So — it may be hinted — our English climate sometimes overdoes its passion for the unexpected. Eighty-four in the shade in October, five degrees of frost in August; a little violent, a thought Futurist?

ST. GEORGE AND THE DRAGON

*

On the twenty-third of this month of April, we keep the feast-day of our Patron Saint — St. George for Merry England. Some of us are inclined to grumble about St. George. In the most respectable Church quarters the opinion has been expressed that it is a pity that the Patron of England is at the best misty, and at the worst mythological. Putting on one side Gibbon's slander, that the St. George of fact was a profiteering if not a swindling contractor to the Roman army — and really there seems every reason to suppose that this was only Gibbon's mischief — nothing remains about St. George but the Dragon. And when it comes to dragons, you know — to put the matter in the manner of Mr. George Sampson — really, you know, upon your life you mustn't. Dragons won't do. And you take away the dragon-killing, really there is nothing left. The compilers of the Roman Breviary did not live in what is called a critical age. They were certainly not men to scan the acts and legends of the saints with a glance of sour incredulity and suspicion; but they can make nothing, or next to nothing, of St. George. The Collect speaks of him as a Martyr without any specific detail, the verses and responses are from the 'Common of Martyrs' — such as are used for all martyrs. There is no legend; no hint that there was a dragon in the case.

Well, that being so, the Roman Breviary evidently knowing nothing whatever about St. George, we may conclude that there is nothing to be known. Our Patron Saint is a shadowy figure. And yet he is vitally interesting — to me at all events. For though the martyr of the third century did not kill any dragons, somebody did kill dragons at that vaguer date known as once upon a time. We know nothing about St. George; but the popular tradition that he was a dragon-killer proves that a very long time ago there were dragons and that there were men who encountered them and killed them. For tradition is always true. It rather understates than exaggerates. In this specific case, for example; go to your cabinet of rarities and curiosities, press the hidden pin, cause the secret drawers in which the rarest things lie to fly open; and take out a golden sovereign. Look at the figure of the dragon which the Saint is riding down and destroying. A horrid-look-

ing brute, certainly; but a pet lamb, a positive
kitten compared with the dragon as it really
was. As it really was? Certainly; only the
scientific people call dragons pterodactyls.
As Kingsley observes, very pleasantly, in *The
Water Babies*, the learned men had been
scoffing at the mere notion of dragons for
long years. Then they found their bones, and
instead of owning up like decent fellows, and
acknowledging that the simple old tale was a
true tale, that there really had been dragons on
the earth, they made up a Greek word and
spoke of pterodactyls, or 'winged fingers' — a
stupid term and not nearly so expressive as
dragons. And, what is more, we know exactly
what these terrific beasts — fifty feet long or
more — looked like; not by the learned recon-
structions of their frames, but in a much more
vivid way. There remains to this day an
exact model, on a huge scale, of the dragon of
the slime. Not as he appeared in the soaring of
his awful flight, beating the air with his 'winged
fingers,' but as he lay torpid, reposing on the
earth. This model is to be seen in Wales. The
Peninsula of Gower, Glamorgan, runs out into
the Bristol Channel. I have often looked at it,
across the water, from the south Pembroke-

shire coast. Carrying the eye from the horrid factory chimneys of Llanelly and Burry Port, you see an undulating range of hills running out south by west. The skyline of these hills swells upwards into a kind of gentle hump at about the middle of the range, and then curving down, ends in an insignificant point, low on the water. A singular shape this point; to the eye it seems curiously flattened: and its name is The Worm's Head. It is not a bit like the head of the worm that the gardener slices with his spade; but 'worm' was old English for dragon; and these swelling hills, ending in a small promontory, must form an exact picture of the horrible pterodactyl, half reptile, half bird, huge in body, ridiculous in head, as it lay at length on the ground. Here, in hill and rock, you have a picture — it is rather an awful thought — of the image in the mind and eye of a prehistoric ancestor who may have lived 400,000 years ago. He had looked into the place of dragons, and had noted the likeness of the monsters to that line of hills running out into the sea; and, somehow, his thought has come down through the tremendous ages; even to our day.

Tradition is always in the right. And, still

occupying ourselves with the St. George legend, another proof can be gathered of the accuracy of the age-long memory of man. There is a picture of St. George and the Dragon, I think by a master of the Venetian school, in which the monster has quite a different aspect from the 'worm' or pterodactyl which gave its name to the Worm's Head. In this picture, the dragon is a horrible bloated beast with a swollen, misshapen body. The painter could never have had a model; but he painted an excellent likeness of an iguanodon, another of those huge monsters that roamed the earth before the earth had boiled and flooded and dried and frozen into the shape that it now bears. Somehow, it seems clear, the word was passed on from age to age across all the gulfs and chasms of time. Where the seas are now, then was dry land; vast Atlantis, the island continent, had not sunken under the waves; there were terrors on the earth indeed – but not the terror of the Channel Passage, since men walked dryfoot from the points known to us as Dover and Calais. The earth heaved, as I say, and boiled; islands rose out of the sea, ships now sail over primæval mountain tops; Europe became a sheet of ice; yet the word was passed on, so that the Pembroke countryman and the Venetian painter knew what dragons were like; both the long breed and the thick breed.

By the way, I wonder whether the members of the Prehistoric Ladies' Toy Dragon Club got on well together? But the consideration of this deep and obscure problem must be postponed for the present.

The memory of man, then, is boundless, reaching back to inconceivable antiquity. It is no marvel, therefore, if it has retained events and circumstances of historic and measurable times. A thousand years, two thousand years are trifling periods indeed when we compare them with the huge, unimaginable chaos of time; still, I remember being amazed when an Oxfordshire farm labourer, who had never been to school and could neither read nor write, said casually to me:

'Ay, Chalgrove Field, that's where they killed Muster Hampden. *They do say it was down in oats at the time.*'

Down in oats at the time! I could almost hear the brushing and rushing of the Cavaliers' chargers, as they trampled down that field of oats in their hot onset.

'And then,' old Harmon went on, 'Squire

Scoop down at Wormsley there; he got hanged when it was all over.'

The name was not quite accurate. He was speaking of the Roundhead Colonel, Adrian Scrope, who was one of the few persons excepted by the merciful Charles II from the Act of Indemnity. To the old countryman it was all actual, gossip of the neighbouring country-side. To be sure, it was only two hundred and fifty years or so since it happened.

And then, I remember reading – I think in *The Guardian* – an interesting article on Tewkes-bury and its Minster. The writer described a visit he had paid to the place thirty years be-fore. He was shown over the church by a verger who ran over the associations of the place, after the manner of most vergers. But presently the visitor became aware that the old fellow was talking quite differently from most vergers. He was speaking of the battle of Tewkesbury; and he talked as if he had been there! He told of little things which do not get into the history books, he described the upper room in a house in the town where cer-tain princes were murdered, and he ended up with a ghastly description of how the dead were brought from the battlefield and brought into the church, 'till the bodies reached up to the top of those pillars.' It was the vivid picture of an onlooker. The visitor made his inquiries, and found that the old man came of a family who had supplied sacristans, clerks, vergers to Tewkesbury Minster from the fifteenth century onward. The verger was telling the tale that his father had told him. And there are odd stories from Scotland and Ireland. In Scotland the simple country people had a silly tale of a knight all in silver armour who was buried under a certain mound on a hillside. Everybody laughed; till some one passing by the mound – eighty or perhaps a hundred years ago – noticed that the ground had been recently disturbed. The antiquaries took the matter in hand. But they were too late. A wisely credulous villager had been before them. Only the knight's bones and one or two laminæ of the wonderful silver armour remained. It was all true; the armour was Danish, dating back to the year 900 or so; the Hamlet period. The tradition had lasted among the unlearned for nine hundred years. And in Ireland the tale was of a fairy rath or castle; a rounded hill from which, said the peasants, flames could be seen issuing of nights. Again tradition was right; flames could have been seen issuing at night from the top of that queer hill; could have been seen, that is, if you happened to have been strolling that way somewhere about A.D 850. Investigation showed that this place had been a retreat of the aboriginal inhabitants of Ireland, the dark 'little people,' and had been sacked by Danes sometime in the ninth century. And as to the flames; the flue to carry off the smoke from the fairy fire was duly discovered.

It is wonderful, all this; but it is all over. I doubt whether old Harmon's children know anything about the culture of Chalgrove Field where Hampden fell; they went to school, the place where ignorance of everything that matters is so carefully imparted. And so with the story of Tewkesbury; the writer of the article visited the place a second time and found a strange verger. *This* man had never seen the stricken field of Tewkesbury, or the blood running in the upper room, or the dead men piled capital-high in the church. He told the story as it was printed in the Guide. The old folk-memory is dead; we have killed it with our silly schools and our rubbishy books.

THE POOR VICTORIANS

WE all know what the poor Victorians were like. We have heard all about them over and over again. To begin with, they were prim. They were proper. They always went to bed early. Their only form of revelry consisted in tea-parties. The laws of their lives were dictated to them by maiden ladies and the vicar's wife. When the maiden ladies and the vicar's wife said that so-and-so was 'not quite nice,' or 'not at all the kind of thing that we expect to meet with in Dulchester,' there was an end of it, whatever 'it' was. Profligacy – displayed, let us say, by smoking a cigar in the High Street – was reproved, and genius, if it had said anything contrary to the maiden standard of Dulchester, thenceforth held its peace. So much for life; as for the arts in the Victorian era; they could not properly be said to exist. Here, too, the ladies of Dulchester were all mighty. Nobody spoke out; nobody dared to be 'daring.' No picture was painted that went beyond the vision of the Young Person. No poem that the Curate might possibly dislike was ever written. If you were at heart a

gay dog you must keep your gaiety dark; else
the County would reject you. If you were a
moral sort of fellow and had an inclination to
rebuke vice, you had to hold your tongue
equally; since vice and immorality and all that
sort of thing were not so much as to be mentioned. You were not to know that such
things existed; since the existence of such
things was not recognized at Miss Pinkerton's
Academy for Young Ladies, and what those
young ladies did not know, nobody was supposed to know. As to love; the word was,
beware! Above all there must be no faintest
hint of the vital things, of any sort of realities.
You might be weakly sentimental, but you must
never be fervid. You must not have 'ideas.'
You must never stray for one moment from
the pink-and-white drawing-room carpet. The
convention was laid strictly down for you and
no Victorian ever thought of departing from
it. And then, all questions of morality and
passion apart, the Victorian author was strictly
required to keep his pages free of everything
'disagreeable' or 'unpleasant.' After all, the
great rule applied here as everywhere else;
he was not to write anything that he would
hesitate to utter in the Vicarage drawing-room

full of maiden ladies and curates and Young Persons. One did not in this sacred place talk about disagreeable things; equally one must not write about them. And so on, and so on; the general conclusion being that the Victorians couldn't write, couldn't paint, couldn't think, and couldn't properly be said to be alive at all. They lived and moved in a world of prim, feeble, old-maidish, curatical, school-girlish pretences, their chief object being to avoid telling or hearing the truth about any subject whatever.

There you are, with your accepted and recognized picture of the Victorian Age. And is it not enough to make one despair of all history? If this nonsense can be written and believed of a period close to our own of a time which many of us remember perfectly well, of an age which has left a great body of documents behind it; if this mendacious rubbish, I say, can pass current as fact; what *is* the good of trying to find out what life was like in the seventeenth century, or in the seventh century? If the near is so hopelessly misrepresented, how will it fare with the remote? For, to come to the documents; this is the manner in which one of the mild Victorian poets wrote of the passion of love.

O Love, Love, Love! O withering might!
O sun that from thy noonday height
Shudderest when I strain my sight,
Throbbing thro' all thy heat and light.
　　Lo, falling from my constant mind,
　　Lo, parch'd and wither'd, deaf and blind,
　　I whirl like leaves in roaring wind.
Last night, when some one spoke his name,
From my swift blood that went and came
A thousand little shafts of flame
Were shiver'd in my narrow frame.
　　O Love, O fire! once he drew
　　With one long kiss my whole soul thro'
　　My lips, as sunlight drinketh dew.

Thus wrote Victorian Tennyson. It does not
remind me of Miss Pinkerton's Academy or the
Vicarage drawing-room.

　　A little solemn, do you think? Well, let us try

　　　Lazy, laughing, languid Jenny
　　　Fond of a kiss and fond of a guinea.
　　　. . . Poor shameful Jenny, full of grace
　　　Thus with your head upon my knee:
　　　Whose person or whose purse may be
　　　The lodestar of your reverie?

Pretty well, in the way of frankness, it seems to

me. The lines are the work of an eminent mid-Victorian, Dante Gabriel Rossetti. And anybody who is not satisfied may be referred to the first series of *Poems and Ballads*, by another eminent mid-Victorian, Algernon Charles Swinburne. And then, as to that other well-known Victorian rule, that you must never mention anything that is not quite nice: listen to this. A well-known character in a novel of this prim age was sent to request the loan of a knife and fork.

'Captain Hopkins lent me the knife and fork, with his compliments to Mr. Micawber. There was a very dirty lady in his little room, and two wan girls, his daughters, with shock heads of hair. I thought it was better to borrow Captain Hopkins' knife and fork, than Captain Hopkins' comb.'

That is not nice, but it was written by Charles Dickens. And do you know the same author's description of the birth of Little Dorrit? The midwife is speaking.

'The flies trouble you, don't they, my dear?' said Mrs. Bangham. 'But p'raps they'll take your mind off it, and do you good. What between the buryin' ground, the grocers, the wagon-stables, and the paunch trade, the Marshalsea flies gets very large. P'raps they're sent as a consolation, if we only know'd it. How are you now, my dear? No better? No, my dear, it ain't to be expected; you'll be worse before you're better, and you know it, don't you? Yes.'

Really, you know, this account of a confinement in a gaol, with all its nauseous circumstances, is by no means prim, curatical, or old-maidish. It does not at all fit in with the picture of the pink-and-white drawing-room in which the souls and bodies of the Victorians are supposed, in popular belief, to have dwelt.

And the Victorians all went to bed early after a cup of weak tea? Did they! I have just turned up a mid-Victorian magazine, *The Welcome Guest*, published in 1858. I open it at a picture: 'Midnight: Supper Rooms in the Haymarket.' It illustrates George Augustus Sala's 'Twice Round the Clock,' and the text tells how the playgoers pour out of the theatres and pour into the Haymarket to eat expensive French dishes, to drink Clos Vougeot, Lafitte and 'Chambertin with yellow seal'; to eat chops, steaks, kidneys, sausages or Welsh rabbit 'washed down by the homely British brown stout, and followed, perchance, by the soothing cigar and the jorum of hot anything and water'; but above all to eat oysters. Why, in our mad daring days the mere cigar purchased at midnight is a criminal offence; and as to Burgundy, stout and 'something hot,' all *that* is a Star Chamber matter.

And be it remembered, these Haymarket supper-rooms were the early places for people who wanted to get home in good time. For the real amateurs of supper there was Evans', and one o'clock was the time to go to Evans', if you would sup like a man. You took a few oysters at the Haymarket, but that as a mere whet to the appetite. Great people have always had strong stomachs, says Sala — in italics — and forthwith he tells us how men supped in the mid-Victorian age; he described the mountains of kidneys, chops, sausages, the pints of stout, the creaming Scotch ale, the mighty measures of punch and grog; and all this beginning at one o'clock in the morning.

So it was in prim 1858; and we, we mad Georgian revellers, we may not buy so much as a cigarette after eight o'clock at night.

The truth is, of course, that the Victorian age, more especially the early and mid-Victorian ages, were times of jollity, and times of liberty, both in life and in letters. Those people who took a dozen oysters in the Haymarket at midnight and strolled off to Covent Garden to eat great suppers at Evans' would not have believed that their grandsons would submit to be smacked and sent to bed early like naughty children. And as in life, so in letters. What the mid-Victorians wrote, whether it were well or ill, was written with a relish. We have lost all that. For Evans' and his 'jolly suppers, his brown stout and his hot grog to follow' at one, two, three in the morning; what have we? The subterranean night-club, mean, debauched, futile, bloodless, the places where adulterated whisky is called 'ginger ale,' and drunk in coffee cups with an air of tremendous devilry, where the guests are spectres of the gutter, dissolute reptiles destitute utterly of all mirth, all gaiety and all jollity, where silly flappers get their 'snow,' and set the first scene of their squalid little tragedies. Jolly? Why, a mortuary is a gay scene by comparison.

And so with art and letters. Cubism, Vorticism, Post-Impressionism; verse that doesn't scan and doesn't rhyme; novels that make one think of a stupid post-mortem or a dull dissection; this is what we have in place of Tennyson, Swinburne, Rossetti, Dickens, Thackeray, the Pre-Raphaelites, and the great illustrators of the despised age, the wood-engravers whose work has become to us miraculous.

Those poor Victorians!

★

THE two most extravagant and improbable books in the world are Euclid and the *Arabian Nights;* but of the two by far the more improbable and extravagant is Euclid. Nay, it is flattery to say that Euclid is improbable; it is impossible.

For, consider; it is highly improbable, no doubt, that by rubbing a lamp you can summon a spirit, or jinn, who will build you a palace of incredible splendour in a night. This is most unlikely, I confess, but I cannot say that it is impossible, simply because neither I nor any one else can pretend to know all the laws of the universe. We are entitled to say that we have never come across the lamp, the genie or the palace; and that we have no intention of believing in the story till it be supported by strong evidence. We can say that, but we are really not entitled to say any more. We mustn't even say 'nonsense!' or 'rubbish!' that is if we are cautious people. For — how long ago is it; twenty years, thirty years? — the state of a gentleman's mind was once in some doubt. His relations were afraid that he was going mad, so they took out what Mr. Sampson Brass called a pretty little commission *de lunatico*. And a mental expert who gave evidence said that in his opinion Mr. X was mad, as mad as a hatter. The doctor had had a cosy little chat with Mr. X, and that gentleman had declared his belief in the possibility of dirigible flight. That was quite enough for the doctor. I don't know whether the poor man was shut up. Possibly he is alive and in a madhouse to this day. He must find it highly amusing to watch the airplanes and airships soaring high above the asylum walls. Then the X-rays. I remember telling a friend about them in the 'nineties; how some queer light had been found which would pierce through the solid walls of flesh and show, as in a photograph, every bone in your body. My friend laughed. He said that he did not believe *everything* that he saw in the papers. And then, you know, 'wireless': what would people have said to *that?* And wireless telephony: before long, they tell me, words uttered in London will be plainly audible in New York. Think of it, the human voice heard clearly across the Atlantic Ocean, as clearly and as easily as if the two speakers were talking to one another across the duck-pond in the farmyard. It was utterly impossible according to all our notions and all our experience; but it has happened or soon will happen. So it doesn't do to say that the highly improbable thing is therefore the impossible thing; Aladdin's Lamp and the Genie and the Palace may yet come into experience.

Yet, as I say, I am willing to allow that the story of Aladdin and the Wonderful Lamp is, on the face of it, highly extravagant and improbable. But Euclid cannot be let down so easily as that. I remember little of that author, I am glad to say, but I shall never forget the astounding statements with which he opens his work. A point, he begins, with the calmness of the finished and shameless liar, has neither parts nor magnitude, but only position. A line, he goes on, is length without breadth. And a plane surface, so he declares, has length and breadth but no thickness. On such foundations does Euclid raise his system of Geometry. Let us consider a little. Euclid is not a theologian. He is not a metaphysician. He is not a spiritualist. He is not dealing with the world of mind, soul or spirit. He is occupied with the visible world that we know, the world of time, space, solidity and matter. And he declares that in

this material world there is something existing
called a point which has no size at all and
no parts: a material thing without mater-
iality. So with his line; it has length without
breadth. Who has seen such a thing? Who can
imagine the possibility of such a thing? And
who can conceive a surface without depth?
Aladdin is improbable; but Euclid is, in the
strictest sense of the word, impossible. His
definitions are contradictions. A man once
asked me if I couldn't think of the Euclidean
surface as I thought of the surface of a perfectly still pool of water. Certainly I can; but
I cannot think of water without depth; and that
is the surface which Euclid propounds for our
acceptance.

So, you see, geometry, a branch of pure
mathematics, the most abstract of the sciences,
the science which is supposed to convey
necessary truth, which no discoveries can affect,
which no experience can render invalid; this
branch of science turns out to be founded on
a series of absurdities and contradictions in
terms. And arithmetic, again, another branch
of pure mathematics; lucky is it for our poor
little boys and girls as they get through the
multiplication table, and advance by painful

degrees to vulgar fractions; lucky is it for them that they do not dream of the nightmare country into which these studies inevitably lead. The Snark was a Boojum! There are worse Boojums than the Snark, as witness that notorious affair of the contest between Achilles and the Tortoise. It is well known that Achilles was the swiftest of all men; *the* champion sprinter, in fact. It is equally well known that the tortoise is one of the slowest of animals. So, oddly enough, their Managements met and arranged that the two should race each other. Naturally, it was a case for handicapping, and to make things simple it was agreed that Achilles ran a hundred times as quickly as the Tortoise, and therefore that Achilles must be scratch, and the animal have a hundred yards' start. Very good. The race takes place. The swift-footed hero flies like light over the hundred yards which separate him from the Tortoise. But in that little space of time the Tortoise, a hundred times slower, has run a yard, and is still ahead. Achilles passes that yard, but the Tortoise has raced a hundredth of a yard and is still ahead. Then the thousandth part of a yard separates them; but the Tortoise by that much is still ahead — and will be ahead throughout all ages, if there be any truth in the science of arithmetic and in its doctrine of fractions. *Solvitur ambulando:* a practical experiment solves *that* puzzle, a philosopher said long ago; but as De Quincey notes, he was a foolish fellow, since the essence of the puzzle lies in the opposition between the known facts of the case and the teaching of science. We know that Achilles would pass the Tortoise in a flash; science tells us that the man must lag behind the reptile for ever.

Now then; to come to the practical application of all this. We have seen that science, in its most abstract mood; in those branches of it which are supposed to deal with necessary and unchanging truth, is founded on rank and preposterous absurdities. With its lines that are all length and no breadth, with its fraction dogmas that lead to the ridiculous; it is clearly nonsense. Very good; *then do not let the doctor interfere with your dinner*.

For, note the difference between pure science and applied science. A line is always a line in all climates and all ages. Supposing there is such a thing at all, it is the same in Paris as in London, in Pekin as in Cape Town. If two and two make four, they have always made four,

and make four as much for Smith as for Robin-
son. But with applied science the case is very
different. Here you enter into a region of
infinite doubts, difficulties, differences; differences of body, differences of mind, differences
of climate, differences of custom, differences of
disposition, differences of inheritance. To put
it in a nutshell; I would as soon go to an astrologer as to a doctor, if I wanted an answer to the
question: 'Is beef bad for me?' It is monstrous
indeed that science, shown to be mad in the
abstract, should presume to dictate to us in the
concrete. Yet it does. Look at the solemn
diets that are prescribed. I have known people
who live — or think they live, for they are not
alive — on nuts, carrots, bread and dates; with a
little cheese as a perilous and doubtful indulg-
ence, and with a glass of milk, if they are
resolved to be dogs and devils. This diet,
which is supposed to be a cure for rheumatism,
forbids all wine, beer, spirits, all coffee, chocolate, cocoa, tea, all peas and beans, all meat,
fish and eggs. If you wish to tread the narrow
way you drink no milk and eat no cheese. I do
not know whether it cures rheumatism, I do
not know whether a wise man would not prefer
to be rheumatic. But the worst of it is that the

people who live in this ridiculous way, who
follow the Vague Treatment, as it is called,
affect airs of superiority. They look down on
the people who eat chops and steaks and thank
God for them. They watch each other. One
of them records how, at afternoon tea, she
occasionally takes half a cup to save trouble;
and she complains mildly that through the
Vague sect the rumour wildly runs: 'Oh, Mrs.
Blank has given up The Diet; *she drinks tea!*'

Then, there is the Bague diet. In this you
eat no meat, of course not; but, furthermore,
you must not have anything cooked. You may
have peas and beans, but they must be raw;
you revel on carrots and turnips, as they come
from the field, save that they are finely shredded.
Cooking, it appears, blasts the vitamines, it
destroys the invaluable potassium salts; cooking is the cause of most of the deadly and awful
diseases that waste the world. Can there be
any more putrid silliness than this? Here is
modern science advising us to go back to the
wretched apish savages who were our remote
ancestors, who grubbed for roots and climbed
for nuts and devoured raw worms because
they had not found out the secret of fire. Even
supposing these pompous imbeciles are right —

there is not the slightest reason to believe that
they are right — is it not better to live like a
man for fifty years on beefsteaks and vol-au-
vents than to mop and mow for a hundred
years like a monkey on chopped carrots? And
then there is the milder but still abhorrent
folly of the physician, the 'well-known physician' of the newspaper interview, who tells
people that they eat far too much; the sort of
man who advises, in print, a small portion of porridge for breakfast, a tomato and a bit of cheese
for lunch, and half a sole and one slice of mutton
for dinner. This fellow is everywhere; and I
need scarcely say that he regards all the alco-
hols as deadly poison. He represents the
almost universal concession to cant. Politi-
cians, who love nothing better than a sound
bottle of champagne opened at two o'clock
in the morning, tell us that the State will rush
down to ruin if we drink a glass of beer after
ten p.m. So doctors, who can relish good meat
and good drink with any man, tell the world
through the newspaper that it ought to live in a
manner that would make a riot in a monastery.

But the *reductio ad absurdum* — I remember
that much Euclid — is quite delightful. For the
last sixty or seventy years, this great bully,

science, a sort of Gradgrind and Bounderby rolled into one, has been bragging and blustering and pretending to know everything and telling its grandmother how to suck eggs, and coming the most tremendous howlers on every possible subject. It has announced with a grin that would make an Earlswood idiot envious that it has been into the dissecting-room and hasn't found the soul there. It tried a little Scripture History and announced, with a decision that the most dogmatic popes have been unable to command, that there are grave flaws in the story of Abraham, because writing is mentioned, and writing was unknown in the period at which Abraham is supposed to have lived. And this magnificent proclamation was made about a fortnight before certain inscribed tablets were found at Tel-el-Amarna; the characters having been formed 2,000 years at least before Abraham was born. Then a little profane history, for a change. You know about Homer and the Siege of Troy. Science laughed. There never was any Homer, there wasn't any Troy, there wasn't any Siege. The whole tale was a sun-myth. It was an account, in allegorical language, of the course of the sun over the heavens, from its rising to its setting.

155

Then came Schliemann. He found Troy standing, what remained of it, in the place in which Homer said it stood. And, moreover, he found that it had been sacked, and that it had been burned, as Homer said it had been burnt. So sun-myths and sun-heroes went out of fashion, and in their place we have culture-gods and culture-heroes and culture-myths, and science is as happy as ever and as pleased as Punch, because it is quite sure that the Holy Grail was a saucepan used for cooking spring cabbage — as sure on this point as it was on the other point; that Achilles was the sun.

Very well, I have no objection. Fools must be fed with folly, and it seems the province of science to give fools their meat in due season. But I say to science: hands off my bill-of-fare! Conclude, if you like, that monkeys and anthropoid apes were the only people who knew how to order dinner. Discover, if you will, that the jackass is the supreme authority on diet, and that there is nothing like thistles. But let science keep its conclusions and discoveries to itself. I am going to have my dinner at the Café Royal.

ON HOLIDAYS

*

IT may sound unpatriotic, even now, almost four years since the ending of the war, but I cannot help it: there is a certain German with whom I am in the most cordial sympathy. I am sure that he and I would have got on very well indeed, on one point at all events.

He is not an actual German. He lives in a book, *The Caravaners*, by the Countess Russell, the author of *Elizabeth and her German Garden*. And I do not deny that there was a great deal to be said against the Baron von Ottringel, of Storchwerder in Prussia. He was a bore of the deadliest kind. He was a snob of the purest water. His selfishness stuck out of him in lumps. He was, as one of the characters in the book declares, 'a very grievous bounder.' He was utterly deficient in all the decent amenities of life. He was a mean cad. But I like him all the same. *For he would not pretend that caravaning was a pleasant holiday*. It fell out like this. Some of the Baron's friends near Storchwerder had English connections, and were making up a caravaning party for the summer holidays. They told the Baron how cheap a plan it was: how a caravan could be hired for fourteen pounds a month, how there would be no hotel bills to pay, no waiters to tip, no railway tickets to be taken. The Baron was a saving man; he was tempted; he became a caravaner. And he disliked it thoroughly. He didn't like helping to get doubtful dinners which took so long to prepare that they had to be eaten by lantern light 'in a gusty place, vainly endeavouring to hold our wraps about us, our feet in wet grass and our heads in a stormy darkness. The fitful flicker of the lanterns played over rapidly cooling eggs. . . . This was not a holiday; this was privation combined with exposure.' And then the poor man had to help to wash up in a rainstorm; and he didn't like that either.

And in spite of the many differences that have separated England and Prussia, I cordially shake hands with the Baron von Ottringel. It is not in the least amusing to anybody but a fool to eat a bad dinner on wet grass in the dark and then to undertake a job for which you have had no training in circumstances of the extremest discomfort. For there is a right way and a wrong way of doing the most trifling tasks, and the right way has to be learned. Even in washing up there are mysteries, as any man can find out for himself if he care to enter his own well-found back-kitchen, with a special washing-up geyser to help him; let him try the experiment on a blasted heath in the dark, with water half warmed over doubtful oil lamps and the heavens emptying themselves upon his head. The Baron was perfectly right; all this is beastly discomfort, and to pretend that it is a pleasant holiday is merely one of the many forms of cant. Of course the only way to enjoy caravaning would be to do in the caravan as the real caravaners do; that is to make oneself into a gipsy. The gipsies, no doubt, get on well enough; they lay no elaborate tables; they have their own modes of cooking suited to the life and the circumstances; they have no passion for spotless plates or for polished knives and forks. They know nothing of the many refinements, delicacies, niceties that have been invented, wisely or unwisely, by people who have had the habit of living in houses for hundreds — or thousands — of years. It is like enough that Mr. Petulengro would be as unhappy at a London hotel as was the Baron von Ottringel in the caravan. But Mr. Petulengro is too sensible a Romany to try to live like a gipsy in a London hotel; he would not attempt to bake a hedgehog in a clay oven on his bedroom floor. It is only the foolish gentile who is capable of playing the impossible part of drawing-room gipsy. Again and again the Baron was right – on the matter of caravaning, at all events.

Yet, though the practice is absurd, the theory is sound. For I suppose that the root of this uncomfortable caravaning business is the desire to take a holiday that shall be as great a change as possible; and this, no doubt, is the real end and benefit of holiday-making. It is not chiefly change of air that we want; change of everything else is much more important. From the mere physical point of view, the London air is good enough for anybody; and our great city, monstrous as it is with its infinite wilderness of houses, is one of the healthiest places in England. It is not our air that we require to change as the summer draws on, but the whole habit of mind and body, of the mind rather than of the body. And, no doubt, a farmer living somewhere Careg y Wastad (Rock of the Wilderness) way, near St. David's (which is sixteen miles from a railway), should take his holiday at Charing Cross. An analysis of the air blowing over Careg y Wastad from the Atlantic Ocean might show it to be purer than the air of the Strand; but the change would set up Mr. Caradoc Owen Morgan, of Llangadwaladyr Fach, for the rest of the year. And here we have the justification of the practice of 'going abroad' for a holiday. We are often told that it is a pity to go to France before we have exhausted the many and exquisite beauties of our own country; that we should explore our own mountains and lakes and moors before we roam in Touraine and Gascony and Provence. And, indeed, it is quite true that there are beauties and delights enough in England, Scotland and Wales to last and outlast the holidays of most lives; and yet there is a great deal to be said for the Continental holiday. Things may not be better nor more beautiful across the Channel; but they are so utterly different. The whole aspect is changed; even a tree on a French hilltop is a different object from a tree on an English hilltop. In our driest, hottest weather the world is presented to our eyes through faint veiling mists; in France the outlines of visible things are shown clearly in an air which is so luminous that the objects seen appear to be illuminated. And then there are the differences of architecture, the strange shock of finding that even small children seem able to speak French quite fluently, the sound of a strange tongue all the while in our ears, the novel aspect of the cafés with the people on the *terrasse* drinking their beer and their coffee in the open air, the queerness of a lunch that has garlic sausage, *omelette fines herbes* and *pieds de porcs grillés* in it instead of roast mutton, mashed, and Cheddar; all these things and many more combine to make a French holiday a very admirable holiday. You have been for a while in another world, you are immensely refreshed and delighted – unless you are like the gentleman I once saw at the Hôtel de France at Bordeaux. It was the hour of déjeuner, and all the company were beginning the *hors d'œuvres* save this true Briton. He was pouring out tea from a Britannia-metal teapot, and ham and eggs were on the plate before him. But I believe this sturdy fellow to have been at Bordeaux on business, not pleasure; anyhow, his was not the way to enjoy the chief benefits of a holiday; change and new experiences. And that brings me to the puzzle of the average Londoner's holiday. I have just been saying that when Mr. Caradoc Owen

Morgan, of Llangadwaladyr Fach, Careg y Wastad, Pembroke, feels that he wants a holiday his best course is to spend a week or two in the heart of London; and clearly the reverse treatment should apply to the City man who is feeling 'fed up' with the City. But somehow it doesn't. He ought to take his holiday at Careg y Wastad; but in fact he very rarely does anything of the kind. He seeks no solitudes, no wild places. He goes to Penzance, Brighton, Eastbourne, Folkestone, Margate, Southend, Cromer, according to his pocket or his tastes, almost always to some place where he will be in the company of crowds of people, where the life of London will be reproduced as nearly as possible, with fresh sea air thrown in.

This is queer; but so it is; and I am afraid the explanation is that the true Londoner hates the true country. It says nothing to him; he is bored by it, he is more than bored by it. I believe that he is frightened of it; that a deep, dark lane at night is almost as terrible to him as is the dark passage to the little child at bedtime. It is a repetition of history. They were just like that in the Augustan age of Rome. The authorities were alarmed. They couldn't prevent the country people from flocking into the great city, and once there, they never went back to the fields. Horace and Virgil, at the high desire of the Emperor, wrote beautiful poems about the delights of farming, and the joys of a country life in summer and winter, of piling the logs on the flame when the snow lay deep on Soracte, of the cool shade by the well of Bandusia in the heats of summer, of the good old days when the Romans loved the land. They wrote these delightful things, but I don't think that they troubled the country much themselves, or Virgil would never have told farmers that the way to get a swarm of bees was to kill a calf and bury it, and Horace would not read so absolutely as a finished man about town. And the country people still swarmed up to the city; and stayed there. So with our Londoners; they agree profoundly with that great Londoner who said a long time ago that he who is tired of London is tired of Life. Perhaps, indeed, like the children, we feel that we are all in the dark and love to keep together and make a noise to raise our spirits; and will not, even for a month or a bare fortnight, leave the cheer of the friendly lamps and the noisy, crowded streets.

*

MANY good people must have been sadly shocked to read of a certain recent bequest which has been recorded in the papers. The testator, a wealthy solicitor, directed his executors to buy six dozen of the best vintage port for the benefit of 'his good friend and partner,' Mr. Blank, in the hope that in drinking it Mr. Blank would be reminded of the cordial relations that had existed between them for many years.

I can imagine, as I say, that horror of varying degrees of intensity will be aroused by these dispositions. There are all the people who hate life, who have many names and styles and titles. They call themselves intellectuals, or, sometimes, the *intelligentsia*; I suppose because they have no intelligent understanding or perception of anything whatever. When you talk to them about literature they will be cross with you if you suggest that the thing exists or has ever existed outside Russia — always excepting, of course, one or two honoured and 'conscientious' English names. If you talk to them about education, they will laugh anything except physical science out of court, reserving always psycho-analysis, which turns the whole world of waking and dreaming into a peculiarly putrid and silly form of nightmare nastiness. But the real mark of this sect is their hatred of life. That is a large order, you will say. So it is. But a lady of my acquaintance put the matter very clearly once before one of the most distinguished members of the sect, a gentleman who never touches good meat or good drink and thinks the habit of smoking a disgusting vice. The lady had been listening to the Intellectual for some time, and then she turned and said: 'I tell you what, George, what would do you good would be to be brought to bed with twins; then you might know something about life!' The lady was proceeding *per impossible*, of course; but I think one sees her point. The sect in question argues most acutely against this, and that, and the other, and argues so well that you are confounded by the strength of its position — till you perceive that what they object to is not this, or that, or the other, but life itself, and, indeed, life is full of objectionable incidents, but it is all the life we know anything about.

Need I say that to the intellectuals, this bequest of six dozen of the very best port will be highly offensive? They are not all teetotallers, perhaps, but they would be agreed to holding port to be at best a very trivial thing. I remember one of them being highly irritated by one of the most savoury volumes of modern times, Professor Saintsbury's *Notes from a Cellar Book*, to read which is almost – but not quite – as rare a treat as the drinking of the choice and curious delicacies in wine that it describes. 'A record of a state of things which has fortunately quite passed away'; in these words, or in words to that effect, did the Intellectual describe the golden volume of one who is learned, it is true, in wine, but learned also in the literatures of the world, a true Professor of the humaner letters. These people, with certain exceptions, always speak with scorn of the Classics. If we get beaten in a foreign market, if the current goes wrong on 'the Met.,' if anything happens that ought not to happen, they say that it is because our educational system is all wrong, since we teach our boys Latin and Greek instead of physical science. Consequently, as despisers of what the Irish hedge schoolmaster called 'the haythen mythology,' these people know nothing about the story of Dionysos, the Wine God; how he went all over the world, civilizing the nations by teaching them the culture of the vine, and they have not heard the moral fable of King Pentheus, who resisted the civilizing mission of Dionysos, tried to keep the vine out of his kingdom, and, as a natural consequence, went mad and came to a dreadful end; being, in fact, torn to pieces. This sounds nonsense, doesn't it? But it has just been happening in our own day. Russia went dry — and then Russia went mad and Bolshevist; and even our advanced 'thinkers' are coming to the conclusion that Bolshevism is a very dreadful end indeed. Russia has been torn to pieces. As for the United States of America, a distinguished American statesman has declared recently that the increase of crime in the States since the coming of Prohibition has been terrific and terrifying.

And, by the way, I have been reading lately about two recent enactments of the Legislature of the Sovereign Commonwealths of Kentucky and Georgia. Kentucky has declared that Evolution is contrary to the laws of the State: Georgia enacts that the man who goes out fishing without his wife's leave is a felon, and that the punishment of his crime shall be a sentence of five years' penal servitude. As I was saying, Pentheus was very odd in his manner towards the end.

But, as I say, the Intellectual is by no means always a teetotaller. His position is rather that meat and drink are matters of no importance, that they are unworthy the consideration of a sage, and that a man who thinks much of his dinner and his glass of vintage port is an inferior person who thinks of meat and drink because he has no mind to think of anything higher. That is why the *intelligentsia* dislike Dickens, who loves nothing better than to describe a feast and the joys of good eating and good drinking. 'This is an inferior mind,' they say. 'If you would see true greatness read Luntic Kolnyatsch in the original Gibrisch' – with Mr. Max Beerbohm's leave. '*He* specializes in skin-disease, vermin and suicide; subjects fit for the genius of the modern world.' All I can say is that it strikes me as a very strange frame of mind. You have something like it in the seventeenth-century Puritans, who hated a great number of noble and beautiful and goodly things; you have, perhaps, the original of it all in the fifth-century Manichees, who founded their faith on a logical basis, at all events.

They were persuaded that the world with all that therein is was made by the devil, and therefore that everything in the world was very evil. A really thoroughgoing Manichee could not break a crust of bread without uttering a long apology for doing so, which was his grace before meat. This was all very well and consistent; but the *intelligentsia* have no very fervid belief in the devil; so why do they either hate, or, at least, despise old vintage port and, in general, all the good things of life? Remember the *Kreutzer Sonata*, by Tolstoi, the ancestor of the whole family of Kolnyatsch. Here you have a book which strikes not at this detail or that; not at the bottle of old port, or the good cigar, or the roast partridge, but at the very source of all life. It is thoroughgoing, certainly, for if the *Kreutzer Sonata* doctrine were carried out we should be delivered from all our troubles, since there would soon be none of us left. Tolstoi held, as it seems, that no children should be born into the world; presumably, therefore, he held that existence in itself is an evil, thus approximating to the doctrine of Buddhism. Well, Buddhism is of India, and Manes, the founder of the Manichees, was a Persian: the East has always been inclined to teetotalism; that is to the denial of the joy of life.

You will remember, of course, that highly popular best seller *Rasselas*, by the late Samuel Johnson, LL.D. Rasselas, Prince of Abyssinia, is speaking:

'By what means,' said the Prince, 'are the Europeans thus powerful; or why, since they can so easily visit Asia and Africa for trade and conquest, cannot the Asiaticks and Africans invade their coasts, plant colonies in their ports, and give laws to their natural princes? The same wind that carries them back would bring us thither.'

The puzzle is addressed to the sage, Imlac, the prince's philosophic counsellor. Imlac, with some circumlocution, gives it up, and Johnson himself, commenting on the passage many years after, did the same. He said that he could see no real explanation of the remarkable facts.

The explanation is, of course, easy enough. The East, as I said, has always been inclined to teetotalism, with all that is implied in that term.

Let us be warned in time. Woe to us if we take to despising good drink while the myriads of millions of China take to strong ale and vintage port. Our day will be done. 'Mene, Mene' will be written on the wall. Let us rather honour the memory and imitate the example of the good man of Gray's Inn, who left six dozen bottles of the finest port to his old friend. I am sure that he was a good man. If a man talks to me of the sacred cause of Humanity, I lock up my few silver spoons. If he speaks of Liberty I know that he has a Bill in his pocket by which it will be made penal to be out of bed after ten p.m. But he who speaks well of port is, as the Greeks said of their best men, beautiful and good.

THE CUSTOM OF THE MANOR

*

THEY have been abolishing things again. Lord Birkenhead's Law of Property Bill — now, I suppose, an Act — puts an end, as 'A Barrister' in the newspaper informs me, to the whole of the Feudal System. A great link has been broken, a link that joined us, in a way, with the men of 1066, with all the life of our fore-fathers from that far-off time to yesterday.

Well, I think it is a pity. I believe that I am not known generally as a politician. My views as to the lodger franchise, the borough as dis-tinct from the county franchise, the several Reform Bills from the 'thirties of the last century onward that were always going to make us happy, as to Redistribution on a logical basis, as to many other things of the same sort, are generally understood to be vague. They are. Extremes meet — few people under-stand the depths of wisdom contained in appar-ently obvious proverbs — and Trotsky and Lenin and I have an equal contempt for votes and all that appertains to votes. *I* am thoroughly with the Parson. My suffragette friend was telling him that 'the Vote' was the breath of life to her, that it would make everything that was wrong right. 'The Vote,' it seemed, was a sort of Tree of Life, the leaves of which were appointed for the healing of the nations. The Parson listened kindly; and made a liberal offer.

'Well,' said he, 'I've got *three* votes, and you're welcome to the lot for half-a-crown.'

Those are my sentiments. I have no interest in votes or in the people who deal in them. But once upon a time I was an ardent politician. The great victory of Gladstone in 1880 warmed my heart. I was an earnest young Liberal. I remember reading in the *Daily News* a short leading article on the Unreformed Corporations. These, it appeared, were certain small bodies ruling small towns up and down England, which had somehow slipped through the sweeping nets of the 'thirties, and now those also were to go. Lord Rosebery, another earnest young Liberal of somewhat greater eminence than myself, had taken the Bill through the Lords and one more relic of the bad old times was over. I was profoundly glad to hear it. And I must make a parenthesis. Why on earth should I be glad? To put the question quite distinctly: What the devil did it matter to me whether corporations were reformed or unre-

174

formed? 'Keep your breath to cool your ain parritch,' Lord Lauderdale might well have said to me: 'Ye'll find it het eneuch.' It is indeed a mystery that I should have concerned myself with such stuff. But I have been investigating these matters somewhat keenly of late, and have come to certain conclusions. More than a year ago I wrote on the mystery of young Blueface, who rows himself into incipient heart-disease at Henley, and later in life finds his chief joy in spread-eagling himself on the face of dreadful Alpine heights, at the imminent risk of his life. I have found out why he does these things. The truth is that the actualities of life are so repulsive that we have been forced to invent all sorts of ways of escaping from them. The Blueface way is one way; the playing of a dozen games of chess all at once blindfolded, is another way; drinking methylated, spirit is yet another way; and I suppose politics is another of these grim sports. If you feel a genial glow at the thought that the Unreformed Corporations are no more; then you are less likely to worry over the fact that you have not had any dinner to-day, and are likely to have a smaller dinner to-morrow.

Well, I glowed as I read this blessed news

in the London street. But, a year or two later, being in my own country down in the West, I read in the local paper that the last Portreeve of Usk, accompanied by his two Bailiffs, had unveiled a window in the parish church, commemorating the ending of this old song. That Unreformed Corporations Act had got to work; and something that had endured for a thousand years or more was ended. I knew then, suddenly, that I was no longer an earnest young Liberal. I knew that I hated the notion of destroying old things, just because they were old; and that, I believe, is not a Liberal frame of mind. But to abolish the Portreeve of Usk! Why, the Chief Magistrate of the City of London was the Portreeve of London before Mayors, much less Lord Mayors, were born or thought of. And I don't believe that Usk is any the happier for having a Local Government Board instead of a Portreeve and two Bailiffs.

Let it be understood clearly; I am by no means in favour of retaining horrible abuses, just because they are old. If the Portreeve of Usk had been enabled, by a Charter of King John, to burn alive in Porthycarne Street any persons to whose opinions he objected, I should be all in favour of a Limiting Clause:

176

earnest Young Liberals, Unbending Young
Conservatives, and a few other people being
alone excepted from its benefits. But I think
it is a pity to smash links just for the sake of
smashing them. Thus with the measure of that
ardent and devoted Tory, Lord Birkenhead. It
abolishes the heriot; the fine of the 'best beast'
levied by the lord of the manor on the successor
of a dead copyholder. I confess that if I were
the new copyholder I should dislike having to
give up my five-hundred guinea hunter to the
lord as the fee of succession. But why abolish
the ancient goodly custom of the heriot? There
is no difficulty. The term 'the best beast'
should be retained, with an explanatory clause
declaring that the said beast shall not exceed
in value a groat, or at the most vj pence. Now,
according to the Laws of Howel Dda, and allowing for the exchange, this beast should be a
kitten before it has caught its first mouse; and
I would insist on the kitten. I would put the
copyholder who refused his heriot of a kitten
in the stocks for five minutes, and if I knew the
correct mediæval English for a custom which
is, doubtless, ancient, I should stipulate that
this false varlet should stand drinks all round
to the Court Baron of the Manor.

And then, again; this wretched enactment sweeps away 'Borough English,' the custom which in certain manors ordains that, not the eldest, but the youngest son is heir. Now, this is fairly tearing things up by the roots. Here is a custom which, I suspect, goes far beyond Norman, far beyond Saxon, far beyond that far, far time when the Celts invaded this island and found a little, dark people dwelling here, a people that lived in caves and in houses, hollowed out in the heart of domed hills. These small people, aborigines so far as we know, are considered on a plausible theory to have furnished the source of all the stories about the Little People – the wise name for the fairies. No doubt the custom of Borough English – under a name and in a tongue which would sound unearthly to modern Europe, save perhaps to Basques and Laps – was the custom of the dark little people of the hills; and so it is, naturally enough, that in the fairy tales the hero is often the youngest son. Has Lord Birkenhead ever heard of Hop-o'-my-Thumb? In framing his measure did he consider the leading case of Beauty and the Beast, which shows that the principle of Borough English applied even to female descent? It would seem not. And yet, how simple it would have been to retain this relic of pre-history, without annoying anybody. Suppose the case of John Smith, copyholder of Mudford, being and situate in the Manor of Muckindyke-le-Marsh. John Smith is making his will; he likes his son Perivale and wishes to cut off his youngest, Mulciber, with a shilling. Very good; let him do so. Mudford goes to Perivale, and Mulciber gets nothing — save the right to entitle himself for the rest of his days 'Heir of Mudford,' after the Scottish precedents of 'Master of Dunblather' and 'Younger of Haddaneuk.' And thus the ancient custom of Borough English would be preserved.

And gavelkind goes too. Gavelkind provided that the estate should be shared out equally between all the surviving sons of the copyholder. This custom, I think, is not of the vast antiquity of Borough English; still it is old and bore witness to the highly interesting fact that in early times the share-and-share-alike principle had its strong supporters, anticipating the modern French laws of inheritance by many hundreds of years. Why abolish it, when it would have been easy to get round it? Why not have arranged that the estate of Blenkinsop should be devised entirely according to the copyholder's fancy, but that all sons should be known as Commoners of Blenkinsop, with the right of digging up one cabbage in the kitchen garden once a year at midnight on the Eve of the Derby?

Why didn't the Lord Chancellor arrange for the digging up of that cabbage? Instead of which he goes about rooting up the past.

THE VICE OF COLLECTING

*

THIS year I spent my holiday with a party of collectors, as, in point of fact, I always do spend it. They are not people of mature years, their ages ranging from five to fifteen. They do not collect First Folios or Conrads or Masefields or *incunabula* — a pleasing word, which means in English very early printed books. They collect shells. Every day, this dozen of children, members of four or five families, comes down to the beach as if for enjoyment. They might bathe in the genial sea, well warmed by the Gulf Stream. They might play games on the mile-long stretch of firm sand. They might get up parties of hide-and-seek among the grassy dunes, up hills and down dales purple with wild thyme, golden with Ladies' Slipper, starred with burnet-roses. The older ones might play golf on the natural links, a wonderful sporting course as I am assured. They might even follow my example and do nothing at all, the best of all sports. Instead of which, they collect shells. As each party arrives, it scatters abroad. Some make for Giltar Head, some for Tenby town, some for the rocks, some for the smooth verge of the sea. In a few minutes the happy party has dissolved itself into melancholy individuals, who walk very slowly to and fro, their bodies bent double, their eyes glued to the sand. Land and sea and sky, craggy rocks and the golden sweep of the bay are all lost for them, blotted out; they see nothing but shells. They gather these shells every day for three weeks. When the night falls they sort them out. Finally, they mount them on sheets of cardboard. And then, the day before the end of the holidays — they throw them away. I believe that the landladies' garden paths consist of the accumulated collections of the last ten years. But commoner sorts gathered with less pains would make as good paths or better. You want about a bushel of pectens to make a foot of good, dry path.

I write, it will be observed, with some degree of venom. But I have always been the enemy of collectors or collections, whether on the large scale or on the small. I love the shell on the sea-shore, glittering from the water, gleaming and pearly in the sun. That very shell, dry and desiccated, gummed on to a cardboard square, seems to me dull, insignificant, uninteresting. And so with the hedgerows, with the deep, shaded banks where flowers of all kinds flourish and grow luxuriant and great and green, with the eyebright and the pink centaury and the enchanting Ladies' Tresses — an exquisite little orchid — on the dunes; with the singular growth of the water plants at the edge of the great marsh; with that patch of luminous blue at the edge of the deep wood where you would say that summer sky had fallen, if you did not know that the forget-me-not blossomed there every year; with the blue rounds of the chicory, the strangely mingled colours of the viper's bugloss, the dwale or deadly nightshade growing sinister, in stony places; with all these beauties and wonders I am enchanted, and on them in their natural places I cannot gaze long enough. But pick them, dry them, press them to death, bury their poor dead bodies in a folio book and call your crime a *Hortus Siccus:* then for me all the enchantment is over. These dismal things are not flowers, but the corpses of flowers. You may take your *Hortus Siccus,* your 'Dry Garden,' to the rubbish heap, for all I care. I don't like corpses. And so with other collections. Years ago a very young man was trying to impart to me the art of sucking eggs with a perseverance and an energy worthy of a better cause. He 'put me through it' smartly, he poured his precious balms of art, literature, culture on my head, he rebuked me in his righteous indignation. Well do I remember his stinging tones as he said to me one day: 'You talk sometimes as if you cared for beautiful things, and yet you never go near the South Kensington Museum!' I hung my head and had not a word to say. The fact was that I had paid a visit to the South Kensington Museum in the year 1880; and this visit had lasted me till 1910. I changed the subject hastily; and soon after my young friend gave me up as a hopeless case. I spent a few more happy years in keeping away from South Kensington Museum; and then one fine day I had to make a second visit, whether I would or no. I shall never forget the horror of that afternoon. Here was another 'Dry Garden'; a collection of beautiful things of all sorts torn from their natural places, their natural purposes, their natural and fit surroundings. The rare and costly plate that should have shone on the cupboard of some high lord was in a case, the chasuble that should have been on a priest's back was in a case, the Persian carpet that should have been on the floor was in a case. In short, everything was out of its place and in a case — except one object, the most melancholy ruin of

184

all. This was, in itself, an exquisite piece of work. It had been an outer winding stairway. It was of carved oak, unpainted and untreated in any way. It was a beautiful piece of fifteenth-century workmanship, and it had been torn from its place, which was, I think, an old house in Rouen. Once, no doubt, these richly balustraded stairs had led up to a doorway as rich, to a goodly house of equal craft and beauty; now they took you to a blank wall and to empty space in the room at South Kensington Museum. I had never thought that there could be such a thing as the corpse of a staircase; but there it was before me; a staircase torn up by the roots, rent from the soil whence it had sprung, deprived of all its fit meaning and significance; truly a ghastly and repulsive spectacle.

I shall be asked, of course, whether I hold that the Rouen staircase should not have been preserved. Certainly I hold that it should be preserved, and preserved in a Museum, for the instruction of technical students, architects, wood carvers, and all such persons. But the general public should not be admitted. It is highly necessary that human bodies should be dissected, that human skeletons should be preserved; for the instruction of students of medicine, surgery, anatomy. But the general sight-seer is not admitted to the Dissecting Room or to the Museum of Anatomy. We do not make a general and public show of a charnel house. Then there is another and very virulent form of this crime of collecting; that is the collecting of books. Take a notorious instance; the First Folio of Shakespeare. What on earth does anybody want with a copy of the First Folio? It is a thoroughly ugly book, vilely printed from a very poor fount on indifferent paper. It is quite difficult to read the text, which is choked with printer's errors. Its size makes it thoroughly unhandy. If you possess a copy you must keep it guarded like a royal treasure, for fear of expert thieves. You hardly dare to turn a page for fear of its 'condition' deteriorating. Practically you have to treat the thing as a magpie treats a bit of glass or a ring; that is, bury it; and which, I wonder, is the more sensible, the collector or the magpie? The only person to whom a first folio can do any real good is that happy man, the convinced and enthusiastic Baconian. For him the printer's errors and blunders are a goldmine. Nothing like the First Folio for those who work the various cyphers. No limit to the gorgeous secrets that can be extracted by this method; the hidden history of the Court of Queen Elizabeth, the true parentage of Bacon, the fact that he wrote the whole literature of the age, English and foreign; that he left ground plans and elevations from which Sir Christopher Wren rebuilt St. Paul's Cathedral, Hampton Court and the City churches a little later, that he designed the watermarks (containing great mysteries) for the paper-makers of his time, that he was the founder of the Society of the Rosy Cross, that he knew all about the Sons of the Widow; all these marvels and many more are to be discovered in the First Folio by the true Baconian. I wish there were enough First Folios to go round these enlightened men; I would shut them and their copies up together.

And then there are the collectors of modern books. They are almost as bad. The other day I was speaking of the habit to an author whose books are just beginning to be collected. 'Of course,' he said, 'I'm glad in a way, because in the long run it means money for me. But what rot it all is! You know those little books of mine, *Waite and Waite* and *Hedger and Mixer*? Well, people are giving a couple of quid for first editions, when they can get infinitely better editions for a bob a time. What do they do it for?' I could not put my author wise — to use an idiom to which he is addicted — and I don't believe anybody can. Why don't people leave the shells on the shore, the flowers in the hedge-rows, and the first editions in the booksellers' shops? It is all a mystery. But then life is full of mysteries and, after all, it is mystery which gives life its delight, its joy and its savour.

★

I AM going to do a very naughty thing. It is dreadful to be bad, but sometimes it is a relief to the feelings. And it does a man good to be a regular devil now and then; always provided that he does not let it get into a hobby. But, I confess, the particular form of naughtiness which I am contemplating is very bad indeed. It is called in the nursery 'answering back.' Bed without any supper is the usual penalty for this offence; and sometimes mummy comes and cries over the cot afterwards, and won't go away till there is a firm understanding that Johnnie is going to be a better boy for the future. And Johnnie, being sleepy, readily undertakes to be a saint for the rest of his days. Well, I hope I shall not catch it quite as badly as that — I rather like supper with something devilled in it — but I confess that I mean to break out. It is not merely answering back, but answering back a reviewer, and a reviewer is more important even than Nana. Still, who cares? I don't believe that Don't Care was eaten by lions. Here goes.

The facts are these. Some few weeks ago I

published a little book. It was about most sorts
of things, and amongst these things it contained
a comparison between the general aspect of
London as I remember it more than forty years
ago, and the London of to-day. There was a
particular contrast drawn between the Row of
the 'eighties and early 'nineties and the Row of
to-day. It is like this:

'Now the old equipages were undeniably the
last word of smartness; in themselves they were
enough to tell the stranger that he had come to
the very centre of the earth, of its riches and
its splendours. There were the high-bred,
high-spirited, high-stepping horses, in the
first place, groomed to the last extreme of
shiny, satiny perfection, tossing their heads
proudly and champing their bits and doing the most wonderful things with their
legs.'

And so forth and so forth; with a very un-
flattering comparison between these splendid
arrays and the modern style — 'now there are
some "Snorting Billies" that choke and snarl and
splutter as they dodge furtively and meanly in
and out of the Park like mechanical rabbits,
bolting for their burrows.' And I dwelt more

particularly on the splendid liveries that were still to be seen in those old days, disassociating myself from the people who despise a servant's job, and laugh at him for being gorgeously dressed. 'The man who found "Blazes" ridiculous,' I observe, 'would probably find the King in his Coronation robes equally ridiculous,' objecting not so much to splendour on a footman's back, but to splendour in itself.

Now, as to all this, Mr. Maurice Hewlett, in a very amiable review of the book in question, takes a strong exception. He agrees with me, he says, in thinking that the old turn-outs were splendid, and that the modern motor-car is not splendid. Where he differs from me is in being quite sure that all splendour is a bad thing.

'I fear,' says Mr. Hewlett, 'that I share what he calls "that vile Liberal objection" to splendour as splendour.' He does find the King in his Coronation robes ridiculous. 'We are all so ridiculous essentially that none of us can afford to dress up.' Now, is Mr. Hewlett right? Waiving for a moment the point about 'Blazes' and His Majesty's Coronation robes, and dressing-up in general: is splendour as splendour a bad thing? Is meanness, the opposite, I take it, of splendour, the one thing that we ought to cultivate? It may be so; but if it be so, we have a tough job before us. We shall have to remake the earth; and the expense will be enormous. For if we are to be honest, and I take it that all good Liberals are honest, we cannot deny that there are many splendours in the material universe. There are the stars at night, for instance, they are splendid; you may call them showy if you like; but still, there they are. There are a great many of them; and some of them are excessively bright. Occasionally, they fall; and we perceive that they are, in fact, great ugly lumps of a metallic nature which science can analyse, if I may say so, in a brace of shakes. Then, why do they shine and put ideas into the heads of poets – 'patens of bright gold' and that sort of thing – and lovers? We know that they are really ferrous compounds and not patens of bright gold. Then what do they mean by it? And what are we going to do about it? And how are we to deal with the notorious outrage of harvest moons? I saw one, last September, coming up through the mists of the sea, a red and smouldering fire, a splendour of the night, an adorable beauty. It is all very

well to object to splendour as splendour. But
will the harvest moon take any notice of our
objections? I doubt it. I know it is disloyal; but
I doubt it.

And then there is another case; a very bad
one. Early this year I bought a bulb for three
and six. It was rather an ugly, shapeless-looking
thing; not nearly so symmetrical as an onion.
I placed it in a wooden tub full of leaf mould,
and watered it at intervals and gave it certain
doses of superphosphate of lime from week to
week. What was the result? Two slender green
stems came up out of the leaf mould and grew
taller and taller and at last produced little green
buds. These swelled and grew great and at last
opened. And now there is a great crown of
splendour: flowers of creamy loveliness, striped
with gold, starred with crimson, radiant with
orange-coloured stamens, exhaling rich odours.
Truly the *Lilium Auratum* is splendour and glorious splendour, arrayed more nobly than Solo-
mon or any other king. It may be urged, of
course, that this lily comes from Japan, an
autocratically-governed country, and that, therefore, the *Lilium Auratum* knows no better; but
I hardly think that this will do. Why, even in
our own country, where every one who wants

the vote can have it, forget-me-nots are still very
blue, and, in spite of the abolition of Christmas
by the sturdy Puritans, holly berries have remained of a bright shade of red. So I am rather
in a difficulty. Like many of the people in Miss
Wilkins' beautiful New England tales: 'I
wanter know.' Nature, from the stars in the sky
to the forget-me-nots on the ground, seems
given to splendour. Why should we, who are, I
suppose, a part of nature, stand out, as it were,
and resolve to be as mean and ugly as we possibly
can? Is this really Liberalism? I cannot think
it. I hope, for the sake of Liberalism, that it
isn't. For if it were, Liberalism would be like
the law according to Mr. Bumble, 'a ass.' For,
if Mr. Hewlett will think it over, he will see
that he has committed himself to the 'Program'
of abolishing all the arts. Turner is splendid,
Bach is splendid; they must go. Mr. Hewlett,
he says, objects to splendour as splendour. Then
Lincoln Cathedral, Durham Cathedral, St.
Paul's Cathedral, Westminster Abbey; all these
must come down, and be beaten into shapeless
ruins and rubble. All beautiful furniture must
be smashed, all curious pottery and porcelain of
the ages must be broken to mend the roads;
nothing splendid, nothing beautiful must be

preserved. Mr. Hewlett objects to splendour as splendour.

And then, more particularly, as to men, as to human beings. 'We are all so ridiculous essentially that none of us can afford to dress up.' Is that so? If so, we are in a very bad way indeed. Are we really to insist that every woman shall go about in a long robe of cinder grey, or in dark green corduroy coat and breeches? Is lace to be a penal offence? Are pretty shoes to spell a month's hard? Are fanciful and charming hats to be a matter for the magistrate? Nay, is a man with a well-cut suit and tie and socks and hat to correspond to be liable to be frog-marched on sight to the nearest police station? But all this is 'dressing up.' Anything, as that wisest of men, Dr. Johnson said, beyond a bull's-hide suit, is dressing up. And what about changing from grey to oddly cut black after seven o'clock every evening: what is this but dressing up? Is Mr. Hewlett too ridiculous essentially to put on evening-dress when he goes out to dinner? And again; since we are all so essentially ridiculous, as he says, what can be more ridiculous than serving that meal of dinner on snowy white napery of choice and costly make, with the ritual of curiously cut glasses, of fine silver, of exquisite flowers, in a room richly furnished, adorned with admirable paintings? The ridiculous creature man is to shovel food into his ridiculous belly that he may prolong his ridiculous existence: cannot he do this without the ridiculous splendour of cut glass, fair linen, Queen Anne silver, costly flowers, while he wears in honour of the evening the sort of coat that his grandfather wore in the morning, and the kind of tie that clergymen wore fifty years ago?

The fact is, of course, that when Mr. Hewlett declares that he dislikes splendour as splendour he is really declaring his dislike of the universe in general and of human nature in particular. The world from the flowers to the stars is a splendid spectacle, and the love of splendour is deeply set in the heart of man. The wretchedest savage with a few poor pots and gourds for all his belongings will yet scratch or cut some kind of decorative pattern on them. Poor work, rude work enough, but it is the best that he can do; the only splendour that he is capable of fashioning. And let us remember this: that it is the love of splendour, the splendid robe, the splendid word, the splendid tune, the splendid picture, which constitutes the vital distinction between man and brute. Many beasts have reason, the faculty of using means for a certain end. But only man has Art, which is the love of splendour and the desire to create it.

IT seems paradoxical, but I am strongly inclined to think that the more comfortable we become, the less we know of comfort. As I may have remarked before in this work, there is no reason to suppose that the Anglo-Indians of the Plains really appreciate the glorious sunshine of the dry season. It would take a new-comer from the Hebrides to enjoy the golden blaze.

You will remember that I once saw a man enjoy a noble fire as it ought to be enjoyed. It was a bitter day of fog and frost in London, and the fire was indeed a gorgeous one, with radiant depths of glowing coal at the heart of it, and great boulders from which jets of burning gas came shooting with a hissing, rushing noise, and flames that roared up the chimney. The man laughed as he came into the room and saw this mighty blaze.

'Ah!' he said as he drew his chair up to the heat, 'you don't really appreciate a good fire till you've been where I've been.'

Then Amundsen began to talk to me about the Polar places where he had been, of the remorseless cold, of wading up to the waist

through boundless plains of freezing slush. And
he looked at the fire as though he loved it. Now,
he was no doubt right in holding that if a man
would really taste all the full savours of a blazing
hearth, he must go to the North Pole; to the
utter, bitter darkness of the world. But the
recipe is a severe one, and the journey long, and
one cannot afford to be all that time away from
business. Still, in the old days, people contrived
to relish their firesides without taking the extreme measure of Polar Exploration. There is
an old coaching print of which I am very fond.
It shows the coach overturned in a wild, snowy
landscape. The passengers are picking their
way heavily, clumsily through the drift, one
going on before with a lantern. 'What miserable discomfort!' you will say. Not a bit of it.
I know, and they know, that after half an hour
or so of our English substitute for the North
Pole, they will come to the noblest roadside inn.
The glow of it will gush out into the wild night
through red-curtained windows; as the door
opens the genial heat will conquer in an instant
all winter weather; and within, a fire that would
melt the frozen Pole itself, and tempting arm-
chairs, and firelight and candlelight flickering
and glittering on right Spanish mahogany.

The coach passengers will laugh just as Amundsen laughed as they come into the room, and
the guard – the man with the lamp – will say:
'Make yourselves comfortable, gentlemen; we
shan't be able to get on for another couple of
hours, or maybe three,' and there will most certainly be punch, and probably some jolly stories.
My belief is that when the coach was announced,
and the passengers were packed in the straw
and muffled up to the eyes in their shawls, they
all declared that they had seldom passed a
pleasanter evening, and fell asleep for the rest of
the journey five minutes afterwards.

In these days one cannot do that kind of thing.
Suppose the express is hung up for a while in a
snowdrift. The steam heat is on, certainly; but
there is nothing jolly about steam heat. As to
punch: it is past ten o'clock and punch after ten
is felony. Besides, most of the passengers have
been instructed by 'A Physician' in their morning paper that there is nothing more chilling in
its effects on the human frame than hot spirits.
So there you are. The coach incident was,
undeniably, something of a lark. There is
nothing of a lark in sitting still in an express for
an hour or two, waiting for the snow ploughs.
And putting these incidents of travel on one side,

I believe we are losing our sense of the joy of a
blazing fire. We are getting to be rationalists on
this subject; and it is always a bad thing to be a
rationalist on any subject. I remember one
night in my own house some guests of mine
began to fall out about the heat of the room.
Some said it was too hot, others that it was not
hot enough. Whereupon an American gentleman in company, raised in the tradition of cen-
tral heating, said sourly:

'What's the good of talking about the temperature of this room? There are probably ten
distinct temperatures in this room.'

Of course there were; and that's just the fun
of it. You can only relish the joy of warmth
properly when cold is, as it were, at your elbow.

The central-heating and steam-pipe people
argue, no doubt, that fires are merely means to
give heat, and that since the modern systems
distribute heat more evenly and more effectually,
they are quite evidently superior to open fires.
Now, this sounds reasonable; but as a matter of
fact it is nonsense. Nay, but it is so. Offer a *fin
gourmet* the rarest of Bordeaux, the noblest Burgundy that you like to imagine, in a teacup, and
watch his face. And be quick about it; for he
will certainly kill you, and the verdict will be

'Justifiable Homicide.' Rationally, the wine is as good in old Betty's teacup as in the thinnest and most curious glass: but — we know better. It isn't. Science would assure us that Château Un Tel or Clos Chose cannot possibly be affected in any way by being poured into porcelain or earthenware instead of glass; and as usual where science is concerned we are forced to answer: 'You are perfectly right: but you lie for all that.' How does this matter of the wine and the teacup — one *could* drink Château vintages out of a teapot, for the matter of that — relate to that other matter of pipe-heating *versus* a roaring fire? Why, each example illustrates the singular but undeniable principle that, even in matters of the senses, there is much more involved than the senses; rather, perhaps, more than the particular sense which is to be gratified. The old hearth, if one comes to think of it, is a species of sacrament, symbolizing a whole world of dear and friendly and sacred and happy things. That leaping flame on the wild winter's night is much more than a means of securing that the temperature of the room shall not fall below 60° Fahrenheit. They understood this so well in old Rome that there were gods of the hearth, the Lares and Penates, and it was in their honour that the flame on the hearth blazed and glowed. And we have something of that ancient feeling still with us; we talk of fighting for our hearths and homes. Has anybody ever talked of fighting for our cellular 'Thermidor' improved reverberating radiators? But the 'Thermidor,' no doubt, distributes heat in a much more even manner than any open fire of coal or logs. And yet again, it doesn't. If we were sheep and goats 'that nourish a blind life within the brain' and felt the cold, then the radiator would be our proper apparatus of heat; but being men, we require, odd as it may seem, to have our souls warmed as well as our bodies; and so we choose, if we are wise, the flame of the sacred hearth, and if we are lucky and have a good store of well-seasoned oak logs, it is of them that we build the fire, and add to our joys the exquisite aroma, the incense of burning wood.

And so, of course, with the parallel case of good wine and the way to drink it. We drink wine for its rare savours and for the genial warmth of body and mind that it produces. But we do not drink it as we drink quinine. I have never heard of a quinine or castor oil gourmet who insisted on quaffing these beverages from a particular kind of glass – I suppose it would be a graduated medicine glass with the beautiful figures for drachms and scruples duly inscribed on its surface. But wine, somehow, we desire to receive after a different fashion. It must be brought to us, either ancient in its encrusted bottle with the dust and cobwebs of its deep, dark cellar thick upon it, or else decanted, in a vessel of cut glass; and the actual glass from which we drink it must be as fine as may be, a pleasure to the eye, a pleasure to the lip on which it rests. Here, again, we are unscientific. The flavour of our Bordeaux or Burgundy or old Port would be just as good if the wine were brought to table in a beer-jug and poured out in a coarse mug with blue band and a brown, blobby tree for its decoration; and, once more, how blest are they who ne'er consent by the ill advice of science to walk! It is a very odd thing – the world is simply chock full of very odd things – but the effect of consenting to walk by the advice of science would be to reduce humanity pretty well to the rank of beasts and barbarians. A pig is not particular as to the design of its trough, and a savage who drinks doesn't care in the least about the shape of the bottle which contains the firewater. This, as I say, is really odd, considering that science is supposed to be the guiding star of the very latest civilization. Science is triumphantly new, modern, progressive; and yet, as we have seen, its practical tendency would appear to be reactionary — though, after all, pigs are very nice animals, and there is a good deal to be said for the Red Man. And thus we come back to the paradox with which we started: the more comfortable we become, the less we know of comfort. We follow scientific principles, close up the hearth and take to the radiator, the error being that man is considered simply as a physiological surface, capable of certain impressions of cold and heat. He is that, but he is quite a number of other things, which are often more important to the sum of his well-being. Why, I dare say that science would be inclined to agree with Mr. Uriah Heep. He, being in gaol, thought that it would be better for everybody if they could be 'took up and brought here.' And as far as I can make out from reading that infernal 'Physician' in the daily paper, those are exactly the conclusions of the latest science. We all eat too much. In gaol our bill-of-fare would be expressed in ounces, and not many of them. Some of us drink 'alcohol' — to think that there are scoundrels so shameless as to call a fine Corton 'alcohol'! In gaol there is no 'alcohol.' Some of us are given to inhaling the dubious or more than dubious alkaloids generally known as tobacco. In gaol no smoking is allowed. Outside, we are often lazy. Inside, scientific authority would see that each got the exact amount of work and exercise proper to his case and constitution. Outside, all sorts of temptations, every kind of vice; nothing of the kind in a prison cell. Outside, houses are often damp and in defective repair — I have had a loose slate on my roof for weeks — inside, everything of this kind is in perfect condition.

In short, we should all be much better off if we were to spend this Christmas in gaol. Clearly: on scientific principles. It is undeniable; and it is also, as usual with scientific principles, the Devil's own lie.

*

'HE and I walked away together; we stopped a little while by the rails of the Adelphi, looking on the Thames, and I said to him with some emotion that I was now thinking of two friends we had lost, who had once lived in the buildings behind us, Beauclerk and Garrick. "Ay, sir (said he tenderly), and two such friends as cannot be supplied." '

'He and I' were Johnson and Boswell. And yet I understand that they are going to pull down the Adelphi.

Nay, 'he and I' were just coming away from poor Davy's house, Number 5, where his widow had entertained them elegantly. Mrs. Garrick had talked of her husband with complacency, and when she cast her eyes on his portrait, which hung over the chimney-piece, said that 'death was now the most agreeable object to her.'

Now, this should be sufficient. The place where this amazing remark was uttered to a festive assembled party, presumably with the object of cheering everybody up, and promoting a flow of genial spirits, such a place as this should be a sacred relic, a house to be preserved for ever.

And yet they are going to pull down the Adelphi. Nay, more. After this gay beginning, there was a large company in the drawing-room. Hannah More and Sir Joshua and Dr. Burney were present at dinner; later came the Bishop of Killaloe – did he often visit his Cathedral Church? – Dr. Percy of the Reliques, and several others. Johnson, talking of 'a very respectable authour' – modern English, 'a distinguished man of letters' – told the company a curious circumstance of his life, which was that he had married a printer's devil.

'And,' added the Doctor, 'she did not disgrace him; the woman had a bottom of good sense.' Now, the Doctor was here talking the English of his youth. If he had said this in 1730 nobody would have laughed. To this day we don't see anything funny when we speak of a blind street or alley as a *cul-de-sac*; I am sure no self-respecting French cook of a very few years ago would have seen the slightest impropriety in murmuring in the ears of Madame la Duchesse, as he presented his new-found and exquisite dish to Her Grace: 'Les culs d'Artichauts à la Marjolaine.' But times change and phrases, and when the great Doctor brought out this sentence at Mrs. Garrick's reception, on Friday, April 20th, 1781: 'most of us could not forbear tittering and laughing.' So Boswell records, though, remembering the honour of the Church, he declares that the Bishop of Killaloe kept his face with perfect steadiness. And Hannah More, who might be considered the Church's Maiden-Aunt-in-chief, slyly hid her face behind a lady's back. This was a tremendous occasion. Johnson would not bear that a phrase of his, meant to be perfectly straightforward common-sense English, should be regarded as funny. And so he glared sternly round and said: 'Where's the merriment?' And then he 'looked aweful,' and slowly pronounced: 'I say the woman was *fundamentally* sensible.' I think that it shows the power of this great man that the company, which had tittered, did not now howl with mirth. But they did not. They 'sat composed as at a funeral.'

And all this in the Adelphi. And yet they are going to pull down the Adelphi.

And, coming to a later, though still a most noble age, and to imagination in place of fact, do you remember where it was that Mr. Wardle rubbed his hands and said:

'Let us have some of your best wine to-day, waiter.'

And the waiter replied:

'You shall have some of the very best, sir.'

Now, I declare that that wine, the very best wine of an old-fashioned London hotel in 1830, has afforded me more choice pleasures than any wine I have ever drunk in fact. I revel in it. I do not seek to know exactly what wine it was. But I have every confidence in it. 'Some of the very best!' It was more than wine; it was dreams and chimes and music. The oldest and the rarest of it had been binned very deep down in dark cellars near the flow of the river, almost from the time of the Brothers Adam. I incline to surmise, though I will not be obstinate, that the dessert wine was Malmsey Madeira, older perhaps than the place where it was drunk; a vintage, let us say, of 1740.

And this wine was administered at Osborne's Hotel in the Adelphi. Is this a place to pull down?

But I am afraid it will be pulled down, and that the game of our dear old London is definitely up. In the last twenty years the change has been great; in the next twenty years it will probably be much greater. The world changes

and the Strand must change with it. I suppose
so; but I am sorry. Of course it all began just
a hundred years ago. Many people have been
accustomed to regard our late King George IV
as a typical Tory. Some people said he was a
pig-headed despot. Leigh Hunt, a Radical, was
sent to gaol for abusing him. But I am afraid he
was not of the true Tory faith. In his youth,
let it be remembered, he had associated with the
Whigs — I fear that they left their mark on him.
Anyhow, it was in his reign that they began to
knock about the Strand; the West Strand, by
Trafalgar Square. David Copperfield remembered the old West Strand.

'I remember two pudding-shops, between
which I was divided, according to my finances.
One was in a court close to St. Martin's Church
— at the back of the church — which is now
removed altogether. The pudding at that shop
was made of currants, and was rather a special
pudding, but was dear, twopennyworth not
being larger than a pennyworth of more ordinary pudding. A good shop for the latter was
in the Strand — somewhere in that part which
has been rebuilt since. It was a stout, pale
pudding, heavy and flabby, and with great flat

raisins in it, stuck in whole at wide distances apart.'

And I remember that stout, pale pudding too. In my day, it was to be seen sweltering in pans in the window of a shop on the north side of the Strand, over against St. Mary's.

Thus David's recollections of his sparse meals. I do not suppose that he – or Dickens – was aware that the court which sold the superior pudding was a relic of a cookshop rookery of the early seventeenth century. The quarter was sometimes called Porridge Island, sometimes the Bermudas, sometimes the Caribbee Islands. In Ben Jonson's day the place was noted for 'bottle ale' and tobacco. In 1753 a periodical essayist mentions the 'fine gentleman whose dinner is served up under cover of a pewter plate, from the Cook's shop in Porridge Island.' Men had eaten and drunk roughly in this maze of courts and alleys for more than two hundred years; poor little David Copperfield comes last and gets his slice of pudding there; and then George IV sweeps it all away. I wish he hadn't. Then there was peace for a long time. Now and then a fine old house was pulled down, and an ugly modern house took its place, but the aspect

of things in the Strand and about it remained
pretty much as they were in 1830. When I first
saw the Strand in 1880 it was still intact, and so
it remained till late in the 'nineties. And then
the crash came. Beautiful old Clement's Inn
was, I think, the first to fall.

'I was once of Clement's Inn,' says Shallow,
'where I think they will talk of mad Shallow yet.'

As you went up by the narrow way from the
Strand, you passed the fine hall of the Society,
built in 1715, and within there were green gardens and closes, and a delicious eighteenth-
century house standing in the middle of a lawn;
what a choice retreat in the very heart of London; peace and greenness within a minute of the
roaring Strand! Down came St. Clement's Inn;
and up went the big red flats. Soon after came the
great scheme. Holywell Street and Wych Street
with their sixteenth-century gables were swept
away; New Inn disappeared; queer mazes of
mouldering streets about Clare Market banished
for ever; the old Globe, the old Olympic became
as Babylon, things fallen and abolished. Austra-
lia House, mighty business buildings, as magnificent as anything in Berlin, stand in their stead.

And now the Adelphi also is to become a
memory!

THE ART OF UNBELIEF

*

I HAVE just been reading a very odd article in a
Sunday paper. It is a series of extracts from a
book called *Lord Kitchener's Lives*. It tells you
exactly how it all happened. It was dictated by
Lord Kitchener's ghost to an otherwise unknown
person called 'Ala Mana.' The story begins
with the great soldier's embarkation on the
Hampshire. It relates the odd behaviour of a
cabin-boy:

'I was attracted to a cabin-boy who darted out
of a shadow, and as he did so, glanced at me
sharply, an expression of peculiar guilt in his
eyes.'

The tale goes on to describe the apparition of
Lord Kitchener's mother and her warning; the
alarm of the submarine; Lord Kitchener's exit
from his cabin and return to it, when he finds
that his papers have been disturbed; his hearing
the click of the lock and finding that he is locked
into the cabin; the shock of the fatal torpedo;
and, when Lord Kitchener had pounded through
the panels of the cabin door, the discovery of
the cabin-boy, with a bullet in his brain and a

214

revolver in his hand. Then comes death by drowning, the assumption of an 'astral body' and remarkable encounters in the world of spirits.

Now, let it be noted that the Sunday paper describes the work as 'mediumistic balderdash.' But it prints four columns of extracts. Why? This is a side issue of the main argument – we shall come to that before long – but the point is curious. The paper prints all these extracts because it realizes that there is a Kitchener Myth, and that many of its readers will be highly interested in anything which bears on it. Strange though it may seem, even in these later days when folk-lore and folk-songs are almost forgotten by the folk whose fathers made them; when the real folk memory is either gone or on the point of going; when all the old tales which were told of winter nights about the fire have become 'subjects' to be dissected and examined and theorized over by learned men; when students in far Western American Universities now gain degrees by writing learned theses on stories that once gladdened or terrified smock-frocked ale-house company by lonely English lanes; when the old myth-making faculty was, one would have said, a thing utterly ended; still, in these days the folk have made a myth about Kitchener.

It was not so strange that the Ireland of a genera-
tion ago refused to believe that Parnell was
dead. There were men in the Ireland of the
'nineties of the last century — perhaps there are
still — who were living in the world of a
thousand years ago; and so the Men of the Hills,
as Parnell himself called them, believed that the
story of their leader's death in a Brighton lodg-
ing-house was all a lie, a lie concocted by the
Saxon and Tim Healy, most likely. Parnell was
gone into some strange region to rest and be
restored and healed of his grievous wounds — I
don't think the Men of the Hills had heard of
Avalon, and probably they had the United
States of America in their minds — but he would
come again and rule once more, and as the old
man in the Irish workhouse told Lady Gregory:
'there would be no police at all, and every poet
should have twenty pounds a year.'

I was saying that there are Irishmen to-day
who are living in the world of a thousand years
ago. I have just quoted an instance. The old
man in the workhouse had no notion, I am sure,
that he was repeating a Welsh prophecy of the
twelfth century with slight variations of phrase.
The Welsh writer was speaking of the golden
age that was to be when Cadwaladyr Vendigeid

should return: 'then,' he said, 'Saxons shall be eradicated and Bards shall flourish.'

It was not wonderful then, that the men of Kerry and Connemara made a myth of the return of Parnell; and for all I know there may be old men and women of the hills who still look for it, in spite of Sinn Fein and the Free State. But we of England, we of London with our morning papers and our evening papers and our Sunday papers and our wireless and our broadcasting and all the rest of it – progress, I think, it is called – it is marvellous that we too still possess the old faculty. We must know in our hearts, you would think, that the *Hampshire* was blown out of the water and that Kitchener was drowned; but we will not have it so. I remember that in my very own house, one night about two years ago, I was saying innocently: 'They tell me that there are really people who believe that Kitchener is still alive: is it possible that there are such people?' Whereupon a young gentleman in company lifted up his hand and with an expression of fervid belief said boldly: 'Here's one of them.' It struck me as wonderful; and all the more when I found that the Survival of Kitchener was only one article in a queer sort of *Credo*, as to the details of which I have become somewhat vague. I think that you were bound to believe that the failure — if it were a failure — of the British Fleet at Jutland was planned by the British Admiralty, and with that went a confession of the iniquity of 'Salome,' and faith in a mysterious volume, possessed by Germany, in which all our names were written. It was the oddest confusion of a creed that ever was, I verily believe. For a few days it turned the calmness and the decency of a British Court of Justice into a scandalous disorder and produced a most ridiculous verdict; and then all the nonsense was forgotten, or so I thought. But, evidently, it was not so. The popular Sunday paper still finds it profitable to quote stuff which it confesses to be 'balderdash,' because the said stuff is related to the Kitchener mythology. Note that mysterious cabin-boy, who behaves in the manner of what the stage calls the heavy man: he is in the famous vein of the myth-makers.

But this by the way. I read on; I read how after a severe struggle, after the ghost of Lord Kitchener had the mortification of seeing the fishes tear his dead body as it sank through the waves; I read how the ghost went up and was received by 'guides' who led it to its high appointed place. The ghost was immediately placed under a professor, who offers a choice of studies and the choicest company.

'He said: "My brother is here too. He was once a man of distinguished rank." He paused. "To-night we go to the banquet. Queen Mary of Scots, King Edward the Seventh and Queen Victoria will be present, also several other notables of the physical world. They are all doing their work here."

'I asked: "What are Queen Mary and Queen Victoria doing?"

'He smiled. "Queen Mary is teaching young souls who are very tender and very spiritual. Each one has a message." He paused. "Queen Victoria is doing some literary, medical, and also scientific work. She is a brilliant student. She will teach the higher souls in a class in medical science. Also, through her interest in the earth, she will be the means of inspiring many great souls there."

'We had by this time come to a very tall building. As we entered, the professor said, "We will go up now in the lightning elevator." '

There is plenty more of the like sort: Queen Elizabeth, Tolstoi, Louis XVI are all encountered. But my point is this: by what faculty are we enabled to declare the whole farrago to be, as the paper rightly names it, balderdash; rubbish of the most hideous kind? For — let us be quite clear as to this point — we know nothing whatever as to the ghostly world. There may be people who think that they are quite certain that there is no such world, who think they are quite certain that when a man dies physically he dies utterly and for ever. I say 'people who *think* that they are certain' as to this and that advisedly; because it is certain that they are not certain: they know nothing whatever about it, and no human being can know anything about it. But, excluding these folks, and taking the rest of us, who are willing to admit that the human personality may persist after death in some manner which we cannot distinctly conceive, how, I ask, are we enabled to say decisively and finally that all this stuff that I have quoted about Kitchener and Queen Victoria and her literary and scientific studies and the rest of it is a lie?

For, as I say, we know nothing about the other world. For all we know it may be a world of balderdash; or, to go deeper still, this account of the studies and occupations of Queen Victoria and Mary Queen of Scots may not be balderdash at all. Let us remember: Dr. Johnson, a very great man and a very acute man, was quite sure that Milton's 'Lycidas' was balderdash or something perilously near it. And Voltaire, a very great man and a very acute man, of quite a different sort from Dr. Johnson, would have put Dante into a lunatic asylum. Now, of course, we are quite sure that both these great men were monstrously wrong: but how about the verdict of two hundred years hence? Then there was poor John Keats and his little book of verses, published about a hundred years ago. The reviewers in *Blackwood's Magazine* and the *Quarterly Review*, men of literary education and of accredited taste in literature, were quite certain that Keats' verse was balderdash. 'Go back to your gallipots, Master John': that, I think, was the polite advice of the Blackwood's authority. Yet, we have since come to the conclusion that Master John wrote some of the most exquisite poetry that has ever been written in English; I think we may be bold enough to say in any earthly tongue. So, dare we be confident as to what constitutes balderdash? Perhaps Queen Victoria is really making progress in her literary, scientific and medical studies. Of course it may be said that the whole tale is very unlikely. It is. But such unlikely things do

happen sometimes. Suppose a prophet coming
to those obscure solicitor people, the Buona-
partes of Corsica, and telling them what the
young Napoleon was to do in history. They
would have said that the prophet's story was a
very unlikely one. And if you had told Robes-
pierre, as he was resigning his judicial post,
because it was against his conscience to sentence
a criminal to death; if you had told him of the
seas of innocent blood he was to spill; how
indignant that mild young legal gentleman with
his mild young verses would have been! And
on the face of it, is there anything much more
unlikely than the transmutation of a bloated
caterpillar into the airy, exquisite butterfly?

Well, then, perhaps Mary Queen of Scots
did exclaim to Lord Kitchener as in the printed
story:

'Oh, you should see King Edward's work!
He paints marvellously. Queen Victoria helps
him in his training, and she is very clever in
painting the eyes.'

And yet, we, we — I will put it brutally — who
have any sense in our heads, know that all this
and all other tales like to it are a farrago of
ghastly imbecility, lying, fraud, delusion; these
elements being mixed in varying proportions in

various cases. We are perfectly certain that this is so: that nobody told the ghost of Kitchener that the ghost of King Edward VII is being helped to put in the eyes by the ghost of Queen Victoria. We are sure of all this: but how? Frankly, I do not know. Logically, as I think I have shown, we have no right to come to any conclusions whatever on the matter; we know nothing at all about it or of the final constitution of the universe.

Yet, we are sure, and when we cease to be sure, why, Heaven help us! And let it be remembered that there is this corollary: if we are justified in disbelieving certain tales, though we have no logical grounds for our disbelief, so also we are justified in believing certain other tales, though we have no logical grounds for our belief.

NOTE

*

ALL these essays and chronicles, with the exception of the last, 'The Art of Unbelief,' appeared in *The Lyons Mail*. The first article, 'Dog and Duck,' has been revised and considerably enlarged since its original appearance in print.

'The Art of Unbelief' was returned to me by the Editor of *The Lyons Mail*, with a few trenchant criticisms:

'I cannot deal with the enclosed . . . I am afraid my readers would not understand it . . . a mass of dissertation, some of which I would not ask our linotype operators to translate.'

Such are the amenities of that highway which Sir Philip Gibbs has so delightfully called 'The Street of Adventure.'

There are adventures and adventures, and some adventures are . . . muddy.

A. M.

PRINTED BY BUTLER AND TANNER LTD., FROME AND LONDON